"WATER, W[illegible]

SYNOPSIS

When asked by Tom Chapman to c[illegible]ng his typescript, it was a painting by Leslie Lawrence of HMS [illegible]TT engulfed by turbulent seas that inspired both the title and the decision to spell 'every where' as Sam Coleridge did in 'The Ancient Mariner', from which the familiar line is taken. And turbulent waters are never far from the scene throughout its pages.

Ancient mariner Tom Chapman spent three of his nine Royal Navy years in WESTCOTT but thanks to his painstaking research he presents here the story of her full twenty-eight years in commission.

Although so often under attack from hostile subs, aircraft, E-boats and mines in the various theatres of war listed on the back cover, WESTCOTT bore a charmed life and survived. Sadly, this cannot be said of so many of the gallant ships with which she sailed.

But that doesn't mean the book is all blood, tears and action stations. Amusing anecdotes abound, like when steaming back to Britain in 1940 after three years on the China Station, WESTCOTT took on unofficial 'emergency rations' at Singapore in the shape of a small pig, for which potato peelings and left overs from the messes were boiled up each day. Came the time when it had grown to twice its original size and was about to be transformed into pork, that we're told how it was piggy in the end that got the last laugh!

Life on the exotic pre-war China Station is described in great detail and not a lot of imagination is needed to understand why many a matelot volunteered for another two-and-a-half year commission there when his time arrived for a draft back to the U.K.

Both ancient and non-mariners alike will find it hard to put this book down - - even if just to put the kettle on - once they embark on Tom Chapman's Odyssey!

Sam Morley, October, 1996.

THIS BOOK IS DEDICATED TO
JEAN MY LATE WIFE

WHO AT THE BEGINNING
TYPED MOST OF THE WORK
AND GAVE ME SO MUCH ENCOURAGEMENT.

ALSO

TO ALL WHO SERVED ABOARD
THIS GALLANT LITTLE SHIP

"WATER, WATER, EVERY WHERE!"

The '74' MAJESTIC
Captain Westcott killed in action at the
Battle of the Nile, 1798.

"WATER, WATER, EVERY WHERE!"

The Life Story of

HMS "WESTCOTT" - February 1918 to June 1946

by

Tom Chapman.

Aedificamas Press

First published 1996 by

Aedificamus Press
The Ridgeway
Northaw, Herts.
EN6 4BG

ISBN 0 9511701 8 X

Printed by
The Book Factory
London N7 7AW

CONTENTS

"WATER, WATER, EVERY WHERE!"

CHAPTER ONE

A Brief History

In World War One, as in World War Two, the German U-boat was Britain's most deadly foe. Hundreds of thousands of tons of our shipping was being sunk month after month; until the torpedo boat destroyer and convoy system were found to be the only effective way of protecting our ships. In 1916 the Admiralty started a crash programme to build sixty-eight "V & W" class destroyers - so called as each was given a name beginning with the letter V or W.

Built by William Denny and Brothers Ltd., Dumbarton, WESTCOTT was laid down on 30th March 1917 and launched on 14th February 1918. She had a displacement of 1,100 tons, could develop 27,000 horse-power and maintain a speed of 31 knots. Her length was three hundred and twelve feet, beam twenty-nine and-a-half feet, and draught eleven feet. The complement at the time of launching was eighty-eight men and officers.

The armament was four 4 inch guns mounted in A, B, X and Y positions and a single pom-pom gun between the two funnels. She had two sets of triple torpedo tubes and a 20 inch searchlight between the two sets of tubes. There were four messes on the fo'c'sle deck for seamen, signalmen and telegraphists, and two messes on the deck below that for stokers. On the fo'c'sle were the petty officers' and chief petty officers' quarters and astern was the wardroom and officers' cabins.

HMS WESTCOTT was named after Captain George Blagdon Westcott RN who was killed at the battle of the Nile in 1798 whilst in command of HMS MAJESTIC. The "Gallant Westcott" Admiral Nelson called him. He came from humble stock and rose from the lower deck to command a battleship of the line.

On completion WESTCOTT joined the 13th destroyer flotilla based at Scapa Flow and given the pennant number D47. She was present at the surrender of the German High Sea Fleet in November 1918 and was at Scapa when the German Fleet scuttled itself there in June 1919.

The story of HMS WESTCOTT runs from her birth at the beginning of February 1918 until her end in June 1946 when she finished up in the breakers-yard at Troon on the west coast of Scotland. She had travelled hundreds of thousands of miles during that time and never once had a major engine breakdown. A tribute to Parson's turbines.

Captain Brian De Courcy-Ireland entered the Navy at the age of twelve and a half as a Cadet at Osborne, joining HMS WESTCOTT as a Sub-lieutenant in July 1918 and is now in his 94th year. He was a midshipman aboard HMS BELLEROPHON, a dreadnought, at the Battle of Jutland.

Here is an edited version of his contribution to a double-page feature in the Daily Mail on 1st June 1996 - the 80th Anniversary of the Battle of Jutland.

'I was a junior midshipman, a "wart". When we entered the BELLEROPHON we all got 12 hard lashes of the cane to keep us in our place and give us a taste of what we could expect.

'In early 1916 we were doing sweeps of the North Sea, it was cold and I hated Scapa Flow. We were a coal-burning ship and I spent my first Christmas Day in the Navy, coaling from 5.30am until 6pm. Everyone had to take part. We got a corned beef sandwich at midday. When it was over we scrubbed the ship and then we got the bath ready for the senior midshipmen.

'When it was our turn, we would have to share two-thirds of a bath of water spread between four tray baths, each of which held about four inches. The senior midshipmen had used them first and by our turn they were like pea soup and very black.

'On May 31, 1916 I was in one of the 12in turrets working the distance calculator. We went into action some time after 7pm. During a lull we came out to get some air and there, floating around us, was a whole mass of bodies and debris. Some of our sailors were cheering, thinking they were German dead, but they were from INVINCIBLE. It was a terrible sight and my first experience of death.

'Just after the battle of Jutland I was on the bridge when a commander came up to the Captain, who was watching the flagships through his glasses. The Commander said: "I beg your pardon, Sir, but the Captain of Marines has cut his throat." The Captain said: "Oh, cut his throat has he? Well, see to it, Commander, will you." Then he returned his gaze to the Flagships and, in the same voice, said "Signal, weigh anchor."

When the German High Seas Fleet surrendered on 21st November 1918 WESTCOTT was one of the escorting destroyers that led the enemy warships to their Scapa Flow anchorage, where they remained, rusting away until 21st June 1919.

A German author wrote "An Account of the Scuttling of the German Grand Fleet at Scapa Flow on 21.6.1919" to which Captain de Courcy-Ireland took exception and answered with:-

> "This is very much a German point of view. The British side of events, particularly from official sources, is very sketchy indeed. In fact, it is based almost entirely on hearsay and stories told to him by local Orcadians:- the teachers, crew and children on a school outing from Stromness in the 'Flying Kestrel' who found themselves caught up in it; the sub postmistress, etc., ashore; plus the crews of the odd assortment of small craft, supply tenders, water-boats, drifters, etc., that serviced the German ships. Many of these accounts lost nothing in dramatic intensity.
>
> HMS WESTCOTT was on duty as Guard Destroyer, berthed at a buoy in Gutter Sound among the German destroyers, at five minutes notice and on a slip wire. There was also a Stand-by Destroyer nearby. On his hasty return from Fleet exercises, Vice Admiral Sir Sidney Freemantle made a signal in plain language calling for an immediate explanation as to why WESTCOTT had not reported that the Germans were abandoning their ships until 1215, a quarter of an hour after the skipper of a water-boat, watering one of the German battleships, had clearly observed it and whose report differed materially from ours.
>
> WESTCOTT's Captain was furious and signalled back; "Since the water-boat to which you refer was alongside a German battleship when the crew began to abandon ship; since the said battleship was out of my sight from my berth in Gutter Sound, as indeed were most of the German big ships due to the presence of the islands of Fara and Cava; since these ships received the signal to scuttle first, and the German destroyers for which WESTCOTT was responsible, last; the difference in time is accountable. So far as material differences are concerned, if you prefer the somewhat

excitable version of events by the skipper of the water-boat to the considered opinions of the Commanding Officer of one of H.M. Ships I have no further explanation to offer".

We never had a reply!

There is little doubt that there was a lack of co-ordination on what action to take in case of an emergency such as occurred and the fact that no senior officer was in charge of the odd collection of patrol drifters, water-boats, supply boats, hoys etc.. Nearly all were manned by civilian crews or young inexperienced fishermen and some actions by the patrol drifters in rotation led to some rather weird ones by individuals. About the only instructions that were given was not to fraternise, nor to go on board any of the German ships.

WESTCOTT tried to stop the crew of one battleship from lowering her boats and abandoning ship, by firing a few machine gun rounds at her side, but clear of the davits and men. All that resulted was that they let go of the falls and then jumped into the sea to man the boats. On another ship nearby a fight was going on between some Germans as there were apparently not enough lifebelts to go round. Returning to Gutter Sound, WESTCOTT selected a couple of destroyers that had been abandoned but were still high in the water, blew their anchor cables and, pushing them into shallow water, subsequently salvaging them. WESTCOTT then tackled HINDENBERG which was still high in the water. The First Lieutenant and a party of men went on board while the Captain tried to push her further inshore. The boarding party tried to close as many hatches and scuttles as they could, but it was hopeless working in the dark on an unfamiliar ship. Many of the clips were rusty and some were missing. The boarding party was forced back all the time by the rising waters. However they had to leave her and she sank upright with the bridge and funnels, etc., above water. Curiously enough she was one of the last to be salvaged. Possibly because of the weight of her the ship blew the hatches as she sank."

And so ends Captain de Courcy-Ireland's story of the sinking of the German Grand Fleet at Scapa Flow.

Between August and November 1919 WESTCOTT was active in the Baltic campaign against the Russian Bolsheviks. In February 1920 she proceeded to the Mediterranean and was there at the occupation of Constantinople by the Allies on 16th March. She subsequently operated against the Nationalist Turks in the Sea of Marmara, carrying out a number of bombardments.

In August 1920 WESTCOTT returned home to join the 2nd destroyer flotilla, Atlantic Fleet. Between May 1921 and April 1935 she served with the 6th destroyer flotilla Atlantic Fleet. In April 1935 she was paid off into the reserve. In September 1935 she was re-commissioned for the 21st destroyer flotilla, Home Fleet, but in May 1936 was paid off again into the reserve at Devonport. During this time in Devonport she had Asdics fitted and was also equipped with two throwers and two depth charge release rails along with 32 depth charges. Her galley was converted from coal to oil fuel and the canteen facilities uprated. On the 2nd October 1936 she was re-commissioned for service as tender to the 4th submarine flotilla on the China Station and left Devonport for Hong Kong on 9th November 1936.

CHAPTER TWO
Outward Bound

On October 2nd 1936 WESTCOTT was re-commissioned and sent to the 4th Submarine Flotilla on the China Station.

On arrival at Gibraltar the ship was re-fuelled and stored up, after which half the crew were given shore leave. During the afternoon some went swimming and others 'walkabout' around the Rock. Come the evening they mostly congregated at the Trocadero Bar, where cafe-royals (coffee laced with rum) have been the time honoured tipple since the Brits occupied Gibraltar in 1713.

An all-lady band, on a raised platform, was playing jazz music and all were quite happy until one old three-badge stoker - not a WESTCOTT man I hasten to add - reached out and tried to grapple with the leg of the lady playing the fiddle. She promptly retaliated by smashing down her violin upon old 'stripey's' head. Then a whistle blew. This apparently was a pre-arranged signal for another ship's company to get into a rugby scrum. The whistle went again and the scrum commenced to push everything before them. Over went tables, drinks and all before them, until they reached the area where WESTCOTT crew members were sitting and who proceeded to lash out at all and sundry in self defence. The fighting went on until the shore patrol arrived. WESTCOTT ship's company returned aboard, battle scarred, and not too happy about their first run ashore in Gibraltar.

Then came a stay of three days at Malta where the run ashore was much quieter - pictures, a swim, a pint or two of Blue Label beer, 'big eats', and all back aboard on time. Not a single skirmish with any other ship's company. Time came for leaving and WESTCOTT continued up Med. to Port Said and after oiling through the Suez Canal, where the ship gave the visual impression of sailing through a sea of sand. During two full days at Port Suez few were interested in going ashore as Port Suez was much the same as Port Said. The smell of the streets was enough. After a few drinks and 'big eats' most returned aboard. The next day the ship sailed for Aden. The heat between decks in the Red Sea was intense. The boiler and engine rooms especially so. It was a treat for watchkeeping stokers to take a spell on the upper deck and catch what little breeze was available. Lime juice was issued to prevent scurvy. Salt tablets also to replace what was lost through perspiration.

When the sea was calm enough, portholes were opened and windscoops fitted to introduce a breeze and a little fresh air onto the mess decks. When turning in for the night they were left out and one particular night the mess was awakened by one of the crew shouting his head off. Lights were hurriedly switched on and there was a stoker wrestling with a huge fish wriggling about on his naked stomach. Eventually he succeeded in catching it and pitched it out of his hammock. It landed on the deck with a thud and squirmed around until one of the lads struck out at it with the mess-deck broom, breaking the handle in half. Eventually the fish was killed and it was decided to have it for breakfast.

The one who had killed it was in the galley all night cleaning and cooking it. In the morning the fish was proudly placed on the breakfast table. Everyone insisted on a helping. But nobody had more than a small forkful - it was as tough as an old seaboot. After that the portholes were kept shut, at the least sign of bad weather while at sea. After taking fuel and provisions on board at Aden WESTCOTT left for Bombay the same day. No leave was given. It was at Aden the ship first came into contact with cockroaches which arrived with the stores. They never left but stayed on board and multiplied considerably. The ship remained in Bombay for five days, giving the crew time to look around. All were shocked at the appalling poverty that existed there.

Soon they were en route to Colombo, where visits were planned to tea and coconut plantations, sacred elephants, botanical gardens and a Buddhist temple, with an old double-decker bus as the principal means of conveyance. Heads bulging with new found knowledge of tea blending, tropical flora and Buddhist lore, they returned on board and left Ceylon for Penang as the next port of call. Arriving Christmas Eve 1936, caterers went ashore to buy food for their various messes. Some bought small chickens, one between two men. The chickens were alive so all had to share the job of killing and plucking them on the upper deck. Two got away and a hectic time developed trying to catch them. They hadn't much meat and could fly like wood pigeons. Everyone gave chase until the terrified birds took a flier over the side, which meant a couple of lads going a bit short for Christmas dinner. Nevertheless, a good time was had by all. Each mess was decorated up with signal flags and toilet paper daubed with various coloured paints. The officers came for'ard and gave a pint of beer to each man. With help of the rum ration, everybody seemed to be having a good Christmas.

A party went ashore around tea time, visiting the Snake Temple, full of a wide variety of snakes. Nobody stayed long as the 'pong' inside the place was awful. After this some took a tour around, visiting other places of interest, including the cable railway. Many made it their business to see as much as possible at each port of call. After all, 'that's why they'd joined', was the general opinion. The ship then set sail for Singapore, arriving five days later. Actually, it was Johore, where the new dry dock was nearly completed. The ship tied up alongside the destroyer they were relieving. It was agreed that WESTCOTT should re-engage the mess boys as their own. They were Chinese and most efficient. They did all the cooking and helped keep the mess deck clean. All the food from now on was supplied by Chinese contractors. It was a good idea, as the NAAFI couldn't compete against them in those waters.

In the dockyard WESTCOTT's torpedo tubes were removed and replaced by racks and a derrick. The idea was to facilitate recovery and storage of torpedoes with dummy heads after our submarines had fired them at their targets on exercises. During this period leave was given. Some visited Singapore itself but only took one trip as it was only possible to travel by taxi and the fares were excessive. In Singapore a few visited the Union Jack Club for 'big eats', then made their way around the streets. One particular street worth remembering was where people could pick their own coffin, or have it made to order. This was done at street level. On the floor above, rooms were let like a hotel where those who had chosen a coffin would sit awaiting death. Somewhat eerie, seeing these well-to-do and elderly people patiently aware that within a few days they were going to pass on.

Whilst at Johore the Sultan officially opened the new dry dock. There were the usual Guards of Honour with all the pomp and ceremony that goes with such occasions. The ship's company of WESTCOTT had to take part in the guard, stokers and seamen altogether. The dry dock was of very modern design and quite capable of dealing with several destroyers at one time. On the day of the opening it must have been the last thought in anyone's mind that the Japanese would capture it before many years had passed. When the grand opening was over stokers and seamen returned to the ship and leave was piped. In the evening entertainment was laid on at the football ground where the Black Watch Regiment was to Beat the Retreat. It was a colourful, stirring ceremony with the magnificent band marching and counter-marching par excellence.

The stay in Johore had come to an end. Bidding 'bon voyage' to the destroyer they had relieved, WESTCOTT was soon on her way to Hong Kong. About halfway through the trip the weather took a turn for the worse. WESTCOTT started pitching and rolling around. All compartments were battened down. The mess deck became increasingly hot and uncomfortable with the boiler and engine rooms even more so. It was a relief to get out on the upper deck, risking the waves, to catch a little fresh air.

During this heavy weather, the ship was diverted from her course to find a merchant vessel in difficulty. Apparently her cargo had shifted and she was being pounded by heavy seas.

When WESTCOTT came up to her it was easy to see why she was in trouble. On the upper deck she carried two large railway locomotives. One of these had broken adrift and was over the starboard side, causing her to list badly. The weather continued bad. It was impossible to lower a boat in such seas, so WESTCOTT just kept sailing around her. This was very unpleasant as one moment she was rolling heavily in a beam sea, the next standing on end. This procedure carried on into the last watch of the day. Most of the crew were watching from various vantage points. Suddenly the locomotive broke adrift completely and plunged into the sea. Everyone thought that the cargo ship would turn over and a cheer broke out as she righted herself. WESTCOTT remained with her until she had made her report. The side of the merchant ship had been damaged by the falling railway engine and still had a list on when WESTCOTT left her. However it was decided that she could make Hainan on her own. After returning to her normal course the weather improved. Putting on speed WESTCOTT arrived at Hong Kong on January 6th 1937.

HMS WESTCOTT
Pennant numbers changed to I 47 when converted to Long Range Escort Destroyer in 1943

CHAPTER THREE
The China Station

Tying up alongside the dockyard wall, Hong Kong was there for all to smell at their leisure. In time you got used to it but it all seemed very strange to the WESTCOTT crew on first going ashore. Most made for the China Fleet Club for steak, eggs and chips or chicken chow mien, after which it was to the pictures. All were surprised to find the cinemas showing the latest American pictures, and how very clean and tidy they were kept. Many returned to the ship in the rickshaws waiting for them outside the cinema. On arrival at the dockyard gates, the rickshaw boys stopped by putting the shafts smartly on the ground and many an unfortunate was pitched unceremoniously to the ground.

The following day WESTCOTT moved from the dockyard to a buoy in the harbour, where no sooner had she tied up, than fleets of sampans came alongside anxious to negotiate for services or sales in some form or the other.

Then followed exercises with submarines on the station. After torpedoes had been fired at the targets WESTCOTT raced round picking them up to be transferred to the mother-ship on returning to harbour. In turn they were reloaded aboard the submarines after cleaning and servicing. Leave was granted nightly. The crew usually went to the China Fleet Club for "big eats", a couple of pints and a game of tombola, followed by a walk round Wanchai - where the girls plied their trade. At night the Chinese played Mahjong - 'Hicks' to the sailors. All you could hear was the 'click, click' of the ivory and bamboo pieces being played.

This, with the smells of joss sticks and cooking-pots upon charcoal fires, was the real Hong Kong. Sometimes libertymen would catch the Peak railway to admire the view from the top of the island. Others would visit a football match or the race-meetings at Happy Valley. An every-distressing sight was the poverty of the people. This was especially disturbing in the mornings when returning on board after spending all night ashore and seeing hundreds of Chinese, of all ages lying out in the streets. As winter approached many would most probably die as they lay there. Life was very cheap in China. Most Chinese believed in reincarnation, so what they didn't have on earth this time would be their lot second time round. Many were anxious for it to arrive.

When the ship was lying out in the harbour a sampan was used to ferry liberty men to and fro. It was usually paddled along by a girl, waggling an oar balanced over the stern on a single pin, known as the 'giggle pin' It got its name because jolly Jack returning aboard after a few drinks would insist on paddling the sampan back to the ship. He never succeeded in keeping the oar on the pin, and his shipmates in the boat would 'fall-about' at his efforts to do so. During the dog watches, tradesmen and dhobi (clothes washing) girls were allowed on board. If one wanted a pair of shoes made all you had to do was put your foot upon a piece of paper. The boot maker would simply draw a line around your foot. The following night he would return with a lovely pair of hand-sewn shoes which fitted perfectly. The ingenuity of the Chinese was amazing.

An elderly lady was allowed on the mess deck to mend clothes. She was known as the Sew-Sew girl and was very popular. You could borrow a couple of dollars from her till pay day. She never seemed to write anything down, but she always remembered who had borrowed money from her when pay day came round. The tailor's name was Jelly Belly. He too was a great character and could make you a suit in a very few hours which would last for years. All the washing was done by dhobi girls. They certainly made the clothes smart and the white suits were made 'whiter-than-white' by rinsing them in rice water. Hong Kong was a fascinating city - there was always something to explore. There were shops where you could see young and old carving intricate designs on ivory with the most primitive tools. Little boys would also be carving designs on cedar wood chests. All these were beautifully executed. You might think that the boys ought to have been at school, but they had to work to survive. This was their schooling.

Poverty and starvation were rife, especially amongst the sampan dwellers. These people were only allowed ashore a few hours at a time to buy food, if they had any money. Sometimes you would see them dredging around the ship's gash chutes to find pieces of waste food that had been thrown down the chutes. It was all pitiful to watch.

In May 1937 WESTCOTT's crew took part in the Military Parade held ashore to mark the Coronation of King George V!. The Army and the Air Force also took part in this. The crew marched for miles behind the various bands. The Chinese loved every minute of it and threw fireworks and bangers amongst them. With the Coronation festivities over, the ship sailed for Wei Hai Wei but it soon proved itself not much of a place. There was only a canteen built from palm fronds, but there was at least plenty of food to be had. There were all kinds of fruit and nuts and you could buy a chicken ready-roasted. These chickens were known as Wei Hai Wei runners and were reputed to live off waste paper and cigarette ends. The crew usually bought fruit and eggs last thing at night to be used as ammunition for pelting other ships' companies on their way back aboard. The practice was to bribe the ship's sampan girl to be the last to leave the jetty at night so that small scale wars could break out with other mariners, using eggs and fruit. This often didn't work out as intended and many arrived back on board like a walking fruit salad!

Trips ashore consisted mostly of cricket or football matches, "big eats" and a game or two of bowling in the canteen alley. This was followed by a sing-song in the canteen itself. Sometimes the canteen would hire acts for our entertainment. They were usually acrobats, jugglers and what have you. One particular night they hired an old man, who did a remarkable sword-swallowing act. He then commenced a fire-eating act. Firstly he took a mouthful of fuel, which he blew up into the air and then put a lighted torch to it. It burst into flames -as did the canteen roof. Sailors did their best to put out the fire with pints of beer but to no avail. Soon the whole roof collapsed and that was the end of the canteen.

To give the ship's company a break from exercises and harbour drill the ship sailed for Cheefoo, an American submarine base at that time where the local people still carried out the horrible practice of binding their children's feet with cloth, thus restricting their growth. It was very strange to see girls of about fourteen or fifteen and even grown up women with feet about six inches long. Some even smaller. Ashore the place was a sailor's paradise. The bars were open all night, and plenty of singing, dancing and food.

Until WESTCOTT's arrival, the Americans had all the bars and girls to themselves. It wasn't long before they resented the British presence and made it apparent that they disliked the 'invasion' into their territory. Things were fairly quiet at first, both sides weighing up the opposition, waiting for the storm to break. Break it did. A few of WESTCOTT's crew were enjoying a pint and watching the floor show when five American sailors came in bent on making trouble. At first there was a good deal of back chat, then suddenly a Yank grabbed the table, turning it upside down with all the British sailors' beer on it. Then a fine old fight got under way. Our lads were putting up a good show, doing their best for King and country, but it was not long before the American shore patrol arrived and the fighting was stopped. It wouldn't have done to argue with them as their practice was to hit first with their truncheons and ask the questions afterwards.

The following afternoon the ship sailed for Chingwangtao, arriving there the next day. No leave was given as it was rumoured a war might break out between the Japanese and Chinese. However the next day notices were posted saying that organised parties would be allowed to visit the Great Wall of China, much to the delight of all on board. Everyone rushed to put their names down and arrangements were made to accommodate both watches. They landed at the jetty, where an old bus was waiting. After climbing aboard, our bus started off with a cough and a splutter. The ride was awful as the old 'banger' didn't make much headway when it came to the hills.

There were many farms and fields en-route in which were hundreds of Chinese troops, and alongside the road were old fashioned guns. Some had the old type traction engine wheels. They looked very heavy and cumbersome and were drawn by teams of mules. It was apparent that there was some truth in the war rumours after all. The troops were poorly clad and looked a dejected bunch of men.

Arriving at the Wall we left the bus and split up into two parties. Up to this point nobody could have realised how mighty it really was. It was roughly between twenty and fifty feet high and around fifteen to twenty five feet wide stretching for nearly a thousand miles. The guide explained that it was built in the third century B.C. to keep out barbaric people and tribes from the north. The construction work was carried out by convicts. It wasn't completed until the year 204 B.C It remains now as a geographical border between China and Mongolia, and is recognised as the Eighth wonder of the World. Those who went on this trip and had photographs taken upon the Wall had something to treasure for the rest of their lives.

Returning to the ship, came the usual round of boiler cleaning and getting things ship-shape. During this time further notices were being put up on the board stating that there would be a tour which included a trip to Tientsin and Peking. This tour was to be conducted by a European firm. The price for service men was four pounds. To some this amounted to two or three weeks wages. However, this was an opportunity that could not be missed and money was raised, by hook or by crook, by most of the crew, to take advantage of this marvellous offer. Once again the old motor-boat took the WESTCOTT party to the jetty from where they embarked by train for Tientsin. It made a pleasant change from the bus and it was better for admiring the scenery. There were miles of paddy-fields and orchards with apple, pear and cherry trees. In other places there were strawberry beds and peanut plants.

The journey was delightful, although the place was filled with soldiers. To the crew it didn't seem to mean a thing, but the ominous war clouds were all around. On arrival at Tientsin they had a meal and a quick trip around the place, being due to catch another train to Peking in a few hours, and then more time in Tientsin on the return journey. The train to Peking was an elaborate affair, quite clean and comfortable, and the trip more or less the same as the one just completed. On reaching Peking, the party were booked into a hotel that had been reserved for them and were then treated to a conducted tour of the city itself, for the real tour was to be on the morrow.

Later having a drink in a bar, they got chatting to several Americans who were certain Japan would start full scale hostilities against China very soon. Some of the Americans were pilots who had served in the Air Force and had just completed their service time. Several of them flew against the Japs in fighter planes and became known later as the famous "Flying Tiger Squadrons". The mercenaries were paid by General Chiang Kia Shek and Madam rewarded them in golden dollars when they shot a Jap plane down. In the years that followed a good many of these pilots died in action against the Japanese in China.

On returning to the hotel the WESTCOTT party were enthralled to get between spotless white sheets again. In each room was a little tea pot containing China tea, and on the side a little jug containing mint; and all kept warm by a pretty tea cosy. In the morning after breakfast, a conducted tour of Peking was arranged. It was an exceptional city - or cities - for there were two, each completely surrounded by its own walls.

The old Imperial City was known as the 'Forbidden City'. It had lovely parks and gardens. From there the crew visited the Purple Forbidden City. Then a journey, after lunch, to see the famous Marco Polo bridge which crosses the Yunting river about ten or twelve miles outside Peking. Unfortunately the area was covered with troops and there were piles of ammunition and stores everywhere. The guide explained that Japanese troops weren't very far away and war could break out any time. It would be unwise to travel any further, so there was nothing else to do but to turn back and return to Peking. Later fighting began at Marco Polo Bridge, which started the war lasting from 1937 to 1945. Peking itself surrendered soon after the declaration of the war and again, to the Communist forces, in 1949. The tour finished on an abrupt end, with the crew taken to the railway station bound for Tientsin. On arrival they found that, instead of being able to look round as promised, they were put on another train to Chingwangtao, to return to WESTCOTT. Back on board they found that steam had already been raised. In a few hours they left harbour, bound for another patrol. Everyone expected the Japs to start something and it wasn't long before they obliged. Returning to Chingwangtao, the fuel tanks were topped up and the ship quickly prepared for sea again. The rumour going around, was that a VIP was coming aboard. The motor boat was kept busy dashing to and from the jetty, each time returning heavily laden with baggage and other equipment. With all this gear stowed below decks the British Ambassador (Sir Hughe Knatchbull Hugessen) came aboard, along with his retinue. After they had settled in the officers' cabins the ship set sail.

When she had cleared harbour WESTCOTT proceeded at full speed to Wei Hai Wei. The weather was very bad. A howling gale was blowing and soon the funnels were red hot with white salt encrusting them. This heavy going proved too much for the government officials, who sent a message to the bridge requesting the skipper to slow down. When they reached Wei Hai Wei the V.I.P's disembarked, continuing their journey south overland. While stokers refuelled, seamen scraped the salt off the funnels before applying a quick coat of paint. Then away on patrol in the Sea of Japan. Oiling and storing ship was done at sea, so the carefree life was ended. Shore leave became a sweet memory from the past.

Japan continued their war against China. Appeals to suspend hostilities and confer came to naught as Japan took the view that what was happening in China was her own affair. They bombed many towns and cities and often flew very low over WESTCOTT. At night you could see the flashes from the guns ashore. The Chinese certainly took a severe beating from the air. While out on one patrol the lookouts spotted an old junk floating bottom upwards. No doubt the Japs had bombed it. They usually did this for bombing practice, just as the fighters did for firing practice. The Captain decided to sink it by ramming, as it was a danger to shipping. When the ship was in position the speed was increased and they went full ahead towards it. The junk was hit with a terrific crash. Just about everyone aboard was thrown off their feet. How no one was injured was a miracle, although the plates for'ard were strained and water started to leak in. Even so, the old junk was still afloat. Some of these junks were huge and very strongly built. There must have been quite a hunk of her submerged. The Captain then decided to sink it with gun fire - it would give the gunners a little practice. It took several shells to sink the old junk, but it eventually went down, amidst cheers from all who watched. After getting under way again it was found that the ship was still taking in water, but the pumps managed to cope with it. It was not long before the shrill pipe of the Quartermaster was piping "Hands fall in for entering harbour". WESTCOTT had reached Vladivostock and Peter the Great Bay. She then moved closer inshore to the Golden Horn Harbour. The forepeak was then examined for damage by WESTCOTT's diver.

During this time the Russian Navy invited the ship's company to a game of football and to show them around the harbour. The Russian Army - not to be outdone - issued an invitation to their camp as well. WESTCOTT went ashore in organised parties. Of course, cameras were forbidden. The harbour installations were found to be large and modern. The Russians had done an enormous amount of reconstruction work. The crew were not allowed to look over the ships, nor even the dockyards. But the Russians were very polite and, through an interpreter, did their best to welcome our lads. They looked extremely fit, well fed and clothed. During the afternoon they arranged a game of football, but WESTCOTT's team was no match for the Russians and were beaten 5-0. Most probably the Russians had more time to practice. In the evening the Army took over. Lorries met the crew to take them to their barracks. The drivers looked real Mongolians. After a hair-raising ride the crew eventually arrived at the camp. It was huge! Everyone was under canvas

Soon vodka began to flow - gallons of it; fiery stuff that burnt the throat and tonsils. Evil-smelling cream cheese and black bread were washed down with more vodka. When it got dark the Cossacks lit bonfires all over the camp, then the fun really began. By this time the vodka was having its desired effect. The soldiers saddled up their horses, magnificent animals - every bit as wild as the riders. After mounting them they commenced to show off their skills with hand-stands, juggling and acrobatic tricks. The horses went at full gallop all the time. At the same time the riders would shout and scream as loud as they could. They were certainly a wild bunch of men, absolutely fearless. After this display of horsemanship the soldiers seated themselves around the camp fires, commencing to play lovely music. Choirs joined in at intervals, singing beautiful songs. All were sad when time came to return aboard.

With temporary repairs carried out WESTCOTT left port, refuelling at sea. Soon she arrived at the port of Tsingtao, remaining there only two or three days. Suddenly orders were received to get up steam and return to Hong Kong.

En route to Hong Kong WESTCOTT received a signal that a typhoon was on its way. Boats, Carley floats, wash down lockers and everything that was movable was secured. The stokers were doing the same in the boiler houses and engine room.

As the seas rose and the howl of the wind grew louder nobody could speak and be heard above the wind. On the bridge the lookouts tied themselves to the torpedo sight binnacles and the helmsman to the wheel. Officers were hanging on like grim death to anything they could find. The ship was turned to the wind and making headway very slowly. All hands were ordered to keep off the upper deck, until it was learnt an oil tanker was somewhere in the vicinity needing assistance. Arriving at the last known position a search began but to no avail. Later it was learnt she had sunk with all hands.

Another ship reported she was in difficulties and eventually found, floundering in heavy seas. Her cargo had shifted causing a tremendous list to port. WESTCOTT must have looked like a little cork being tossed about at the whim of the waves and wind.

The seas were now running at unbelievable heights, eighty to a hundred feet or more. When WESTCOTT went into the dip of a wave you wondered whether you would ever see the other ship again. The Captain decided to pump oil fuel all round the stricken ship. It did help but to be on the safe side the Captain thought it best to remain with her. By now the typhoon had passed on its destructive way. The wind had abated and conditions had improved as suddenly as they began. As the sea became less rough it was time to see what damage had been done. Part of the bridge and all the boats were smashed and stanchions between messdecks had been bent under the strain. The temporary repairs up for'ard had been carried away and the Asdic compartment was flooded, but apart from that little lot they were still intact. Soon the fire and bilge pumps were working and things began to return to normal. The cargo ship probably fared worse than WESTCOTT, but she had way on and slowly made Fuchow.

As it entered harbour WESTCOTT bade farewell and proceeded to Hong Kong. Upon approaching the entrance to the harbour of Hong Kong the appalling destruction and havoc the typhoon had caused could be seen. On the north side of the harbour against the rocks and cliffs, was a large Japanese liner that had been on its maiden voyage. It looked as if some gigantic hand had lifted it out of the water, placing it on top of the cliffs. Casualties were caused by the tidal wave that came with the typhoon, causing more deaths among the sampan dwellers that it was possible to count. As the ship proceeded into the harbour devastation all around met the eye. The harbour was full of sunken ships, boats, sampans, junks and dead bodies. As soon as it was possible the ship went into dry dock over on the Kowloon side. Once high and dry the crew were detailed off into working parties to remove the dead and injured from the ruined buildings. The ship's company joined forces with the army to carry out this awful task. The horror of the situation defies all attempts to explain. Men, women and little children were trapped under buildings for days. The dead were estimated to be 11,000. Heaven knows how many injured there were.

Twenty-eight ships had been sunk and many more driven ashore. One of these was carried by the tidal wave through the streets and left high and dry between the tram lines. The ferry that plied between Kowloon and Hong Kong was dumped stern first upon the boiler house roof in the dockyard. All the passengers were dead. This work continued until most of the civilians had been cleared from the rubble. You can imagine that as each day passed conditions grew worse. In the end things started to return to normal. To some, however, things would never be the same. When the ship had completed its repairs and was out of dry dock, the C in C came aboard and thanked the ship's company. He then told them that wind speeds of one hundred and sixty-two miles per hour were recorded in the typhoon!

During this time the Japanese had continued with their hostilities. They carried out a bombardment upon Amoy. Canton had been bombed and up the river the American ship 'Panay' had been sunk by aircraft, as well as two oil tankers. A British 'C' Class Cruiser had been under a blockade up the river and it eventually ran the gauntlet, arriving in Hong Kong amid loud cheers from all the ships that had cleared lower deck for the purpose. She had several women and children on board - 'ex-pats' who had been out in China with their husbands and fathers. Several children were born aboard while she had been up the river. One Sunday amid gay celebrations the whole lot were taken on board and christened by the ship's Padre. It was now the beginning of 1938. WESTCOTT re-commenced her exercises with the submarines and was in and out of harbour every day. As spring approached she left Hong Kong for a long cruise, the first port of call being Manila in the Philippines, where the Americans made the crew very welcome.

The next port of call was Labuan in British North Borneo. The place was just swamp-land and full of muddy creeks. The natives here were very small indeed. They lived in huts built on wooden piles at the water's edge. The main diet of these people seemed to be roots and fish. One strange custom the women had was to smoke a long pipe from one nostril.

The next port of call was Miri, where the oil fields were. The white population ashore organised dances and parties for the crew and all enjoyed themselves thoroughly. Steaming further south, WESTCOTT finished up at Bali with its wonderful beach, temples and dusky, but very handsome dancing girls. After a glorious time the crew were sad to say goodbye to Bali. There came a brief exercise with Australian ships in the Indian Ocean before WESTCOTT proceeded to the Dutch Naval Base at Surabaya, going alongside the dockyard wall. Surabaya was a nice clean place, as were all the Dutch colonies. The Dutch Naval authorities also organised trips by bus to a large, open-air zoo.

After sailing from Surabaya the ship called at Malacca and then on to Singapore, anchoring in the harbour. WESTCOTT was surrounded by dozens of merchant ships of all types and nationalities. Junks and sampans were everywhere. It was a hive of industry, but the smell was awful. When leave was given some went to cool off at the cinema, others went 'walkabout' and a few to the 'New World'. This was a fine, open-air fair-ground, which never seemed to close at all. There were helter-skelters, swings and side shows. It was more or less like an English fair. The only difference was the open-air Chinese theatre. On leaving the New World fair-ground most would finish up at the Union Jack Club, where cleaning up and 'big eats' was the order of the day before returning on board.

It was now the beginning of April 1938. The ship was once again on the move, returning to Hong Kong. When she arrived it was Sunday and, just before divisions, a new troop-ship,

DUNERA, entered on the Kowloon side. This ship was to take some of WESTCOTT's crew back to the U.K.

Back on submarine exercises WESTCOTT was off the coast of Malaya when the accompanying sub fired six torpedoes but on searching around until nightfall only five could be found. On resuming the exercise next morning a vigilant lookout noticed a track of oil on the beach that proved to be diesel oil such as would have been used in our lost torpedo. So the Captain requested the RAF station at Seletta to investigate for us, and they spotted a tribe of natives carrying it through the jungle on their shoulders. A search party was set up to go and retrieve it. By the time they reached them they were some two miles inland and it took the team a week to get it back to the beach. One wonders what the natives were going to do with it. After this episode WESTCOTT returned to Hong Kong being one of the very few ships whose crew had to travel two miles inland to recover a torpedo.

It was now October 1938 and for Trafalgar Day celebrations it was decided to have a great parade on Happy Valley's race course. It was to be the biggest parade ever to be held. Probably to impress the Japanese. Naval personnel from every ship, from cruiser down to MTB, took part. Dress of the day was Number Ones with belts, gaiters and fixed bayonets. No verbal orders were given, all orders were by flag signals from the stadium roof. The salute was taken by Sir Percy Noble C in C Far East. Indeed it was most impressive. Royal Marines, as usual, providing the stirring music to march to.

Owing to the crisis in China WESTCOTT was dispatched to Singapore, whereupon her torpedo tubes and gun were replaced, her asdic dome removed and a steel plate fitted over the hole. After ammunition was taken on board, she was sent up to Pel-Ho river to relieve HMS DIANA.

The journey up river was perilous, for on one side were the Japanese and on the other Chinese bandits. On arriving at Taku WESTCOTT's duty was guard ship for British vessels. Apparently Japanese officers were going aboard these ships and stealing from cabins etc. A Naval sentry was put on board each ship at the head of the gangway with a trenching tool for use as defence or offence. It seemed to work and at least the Japanese were stopped. Because of the belligerent Japanese and marauding Chinese bandits WESTCOTT was obliged to protect itself with guards, too, and take care when venturing on deck.

When finally relieved of guard duty WESTCOTT returned to Hong Kong. As she slowly proceeded down the Pei-Ho, mud huts were to be seen at either side. This was where those below the poverty line in China lived. In those days it was the custom of these poor people to drown any girl that was born to the family, for girls only meant extra expense which they could ill afford. It was a gruesome and pitiful sight to see these little bodies but one dare not take them out of the water because whoever did became responsible for their funeral.

From Hong Kong WESTCOTT was sent to Singapore again where once more she reverted to a submarine tender. Many places were visited that year and each was as unusual and interesting as the next.

In December Captain Lolly was relieved by Commander Firth who after three months aboard took very ill. While at Wei Hai Wei he died. His funeral took place on the island and representatives from the whole of the Fleet attended together with most of WESTCOTT's ships company. Unfortunately his family were on the way out to join him and had to be greeted with this awful news.

On the 1st April 1939, another brand new troopship, HMT ETTRICK, arrived in Hong Kong harbour. Thus begins my personal contribution to the life story of HMS WESTCOTT as, until now, I've had to rely on research and verbal versions of experiences from others.

CHAPTER FOUR

The Mystic East!

Arriving at Hong Kong aboard HMT ETTRICK after a trouble free six-week voyage out, those of us bound for WESTCOTT gathered up bags and hammocks and were transported to where she was lying. Her crew lined the ship's side and gazed on us in disbelief as we came up the ladder in brand new voluminous white pusser's shorts and regulation solar topees on our heads. It didn't take long to learn that nobody - but nobody - wore pusser's solar topees out East - and nor did any of our party ever again after that. In return, we looked at WESTCOTT and thought, "What have we here?" There were no torpedo tubes, no 'Y' gun. We thought she must be in for a refit but were soon to learn she was not.

With my gear stowed away and hammock in the rack, I learned from fellow mess-mates that the ship was an old V & W class destroyer, converted to target-ship for practice torpedoes to be fired at it by our own submarines. Torpedo tubes had been removed and storage racks put in their place. Eighteen torpedoes could be accommodated on these racks, nine on each, stowed on top of each other like a pyramid and protected by fenders. The idea was to go to sea with three submarines, each firing six torpedoes at us, with dummy heads on. After picking them up, they'd be delivered to HMS MEDWAY, the submarine depot-ship, for overhaul and re-charge with air before being returned to the respective submarines from which they'd been fired.

I found WESTCOTT smaller than my last ship; the messes were closer together and the facilities were poor. There were four 4" low angle guns, no director control, no 'Y' gun and the so called gun shields left the gun crew half-exposed to machine gun fire and shell splinters. It had only one anti aircraft gun - a two pound pom pom - which proved woefully lacking when put to the test. 'Y' gun had been removed to counteract the weight difference when all eighteen torpedoes were on board. Between where the torpedo tubes had been was a derrick used to pluck these torpedoes out of the water. The derrick was operated by an electric winch on the 'Y' gun platform. Having no torpedoes aboard, the need for torpedo staff was much reduced, hence only four torpedo-men, of which I was one. In messes one and two were seamen and seaman-gunners. In three-mess were more seamen and the torpedo-men. In number four mess were the signalmen and telegraphists. Below us were two messes for the stokers and above us on the fo'c'sle the P.O and C.P.O. messes. Aft was the Captain's day cabin, the wardroom, officers' quarters and the stewards' mess. On the bridge was the Captain's sea cabin. The total complement was one hundred and ten men.

One big advantage over my last ship, ENCOUNTER, were the Chinese mess caterers. Each mess had a mess boy, as they were termed. These boys bought and prepared the food and served it out, cleared away and washed up. They did all the meals, having one day off a week. Of course they were free to go home when in harbour after the last meal was finished. The boys' duties were to go ashore and buy the cheapest and best food they could find. Our catering allowance was given them to pay for all this and what was left was their own. Things were very cheap out there, so they did not do too badly. The trouble with our mess boy, Mr Wong, was he spent all his money gambling at mah jong, playing all through the night. He was married with children. How they managed I do not know. At least he was clean and well dressed and we were well satisfied with his endeavours.

It was not long before I met up with the Sew Sew girl, the tailor Jelly Belly, the shoe maker and the dhobi girls. It was worth every penny to make use of these people for they were exceedingly good. The dhobi girls would come on board, take away all our dirty washing and return it the next day spotlessly clean and pressed. Worth every one of the few cents they charged, considering all the white clothes we wore. After my last ship, personal catering, dhobying, etc. now became a thing of the past - for a few months at least.

After a good supper I sat and yarned with my new mess-mates. It is funny, you always find a few who have the most vivid imagination, to colour up the simplest yarn. Tales of personal experiences with the Chinese girls ashore were unbelievable and I could not get ashore fast enough to find out for myself, but I was still looking when it came to leaving the Far East one year later. Some of the crew were physical fitness experts, seeing how many times they could pull themselves up and down on the hammock bars but cards, dominoes, chess, uckers, and mah jong in the mess was more in my line. Of course, we all sat and wrote letters home. Page after page in some cases and I'd often wonder where they got all the news from.

Being a torpedoeman I was expected to help the other two with the electrical work on board ship.

The morning after my arrival I went on deck for my first look at Hong Kong. In the harbour and out to sea were junks and sampans by the hundred. The junks were homes and workshops for the Chinese, and means of transport from Hong Kong to Kowloon and mainland China. Men, women and children all trying to live and get a living. Among all the Chinese craft, were Royal Navy cruisers, destroyers, submarines and HMS MEDWAY, the submarine depot ship. Half the China Fleet must have been in harbour. As far as I could see, everyone ashore lived in high-rise flats. There were colourful hordes of people going about their business. I was dying to get ashore and see it all close-up.

When I did go I went alone, feeling that way I'd see and learn a lot more of Hong Kong than if I just joined up with some shipmates to the nearest bar or Joss House. The first stop was the China Fleet Club, a concrete building four storeys high. Inside, it was just like the Navy House in Chatham, except the staff were all Chinese. It seemed they could not do enough for you, but after a cup of coffee I left the Club, turned left and entered the Chinese district of Wanchai and its open-air market. They were selling all sorts of clothes, hardware and food. Most of which smelled awful, but nobody seemed to mind, except possible me.

The dress of the Chinese comprised loose fitting trousers and jacket. Some of the men had pig tails, nearly all wore saucer-shaped hats and a few had trilby-type head wear. On their feet some had sandals, some had clogs. Once, when I stayed in the China Fleet Club for a night, I heard the clip clop of these clogs on the pavement throughout the night as so many of them had no beds to go to. The poorer Chinese wore sombre clothes with no footwear at all. The more well-to-do Chinese women wore colourful and pretty robes.

Girls were plentiful and available for one dollar fifty cents. At current rates that would be about seven and a half pence a time. And although that would appear to make the wages of sin somewhat meagre they appeared to be pretty happy with their lot. A number of the girls lived in flats which were rented, or loaned, from older women, called Almas. Usually the money the girls earned was given to the Alma. In return they received food and shelter, plus a little pocket money to buy clothes. Often the Alma would approach a passing sailor with, "You want brand new girl from Chungking?" on the basis that Jack might believe that a fresh consignment from up-country was a treat not to be lightly spurned.

The next time I went ashore was with my opposite number to the China Fleet Club and turning right this time when we came out after a drink walked towards the centre of Hong Kong along the main street. All about were rickshaws which could seat one or two people and were pulled by scrawny Chinese coolies. The muscles on whose legs stood out like ships' hawsers because they ran wherever they were asked to go. Most had a little knowledge of English. They usually carried a bed roll which at night would be unrolled in any shop doorway and that was where they slept. They certainly had no homes to go to and life was hard despite the fact that the main street was lined with shops and cinemas. The goods in the shops were really lovely, but far too expensive for the average matelot, let alone the passing coolie. After window shopping we continued taking in all the exotic detail. At the main crossroads policemen stood on boxes directing the heavy traffic. At the piers, ferries were alongside, loading and unloading. One carried passengers only and a larger one was disembarking both pedestrians and vehicles. Across the water was Kowloon and mainland China. Further along the wharf, other ships were tied up, stern to the jetty, with their bows pointing out to sea, unloading their wares into junks. Soon it was time to return to the ship, passing as we went through flag-draped streets. From the upper windows of the dwellings gaily coloured flags hung out over each shop. All emblazoned with Chinese writing and pictures. What was printed on them I do not know, probably the name of the person who owned the shop at street level and the kind of goods and services offered. All very strange and interesting but not a bit like Darlington High Street!

When staying overnight in the China Fleet Club you could have all your clothes washed. By the time you got up in the morning they were clean and neatly pressed at your bedside. For breakfast there were small pullet eggs, tasting like fish and for dinner one usually got a small chicken called a Wei Hai Wei runner. It was a bit expensive, but the luxury was worth it on a long weekend ashore.

It was now time to exercise with the submarines. Leaving harbour we were soon on our way into the China Sea, leading three submarines that quickly disappeared under the waves. WESTCOTT, in these early days, was fitted with the new anti-submarine detecting gear (Asdic) which would be lowered into the water underneath the ship. When operating it sent out a sonar signal that would just fade away if nothing was in its path. If a shoal of fish was contacted a dull signal would bounce back, but if something metallic, like a submarine, a high pitched 'ping' would be received. But it took a highly-skilled operator to use it effectively.

At the beginning of the war the Germans and Japanese had torpedoes that left very little trail. We were still using the old Whitehead torpedoes that left a trail of bubbles as they travelled through the water to their target. The Germans had electric torpedoes, which were very difficult to locate, the Japanese had the most formidable version in the world, the Long Lance Torpedo. This was thirty feet long, travelled twenty miles, had a war head weighing one ton and was powered by hydrogen - another deep, dark secret. Watching for the tell-tale trail of bubbles from the torpedoes that had been fired by our submarines the Asdic operators would try to trace their source and pass the bearings to the bridge officer who would order speed and rudder changes as required to take evasive action. In calm weather we were quite successful, especially if there was only one submarine to contend with; but if it was rough, with two or three subs endeavouring to attack at the same time, it was a very different kettle of fish.

When the torpedoes were fired they were set at a depth to pass underneath the ship to prevent damage to us or the torpedo, costing as they did about three thousand pounds each at the time. After completing its run the air vessel gave the torpedo positive buoyancy and it bobbed to the surface. The recovery operation was quite a simple one. The ship would be taken alongside the torpedo, where a line was hooked to the ring in its nose. Another rope was slipped down that line towards the tail. A steel band was then passed down and threaded over the tail of the torpedo and slipped along to the point of balance and the electric winch then hoisted it aboard. The whole job took about five to ten minutes. The torpedo petty officer was in charge. The leading torpedo operator was on the winch and the other seaman torpedo-man and myself were there to secure the torpedoes on the racks. The racks had a series of holes in them. A steel bar was placed in one of these holes and then another was put on the other side of the torpedo to stop it from rolling about. This exercise was repeated until all torpedoes had been picked up. Five were placed on first, then four on top, protected by fenders. Finally, all were secured by ropes.

By tying a grotty hammock to the stern rails while at sea it was fresh, soft, and smelt good when it came to turning in on it after it had been towed in WESTCOTT'S wake for a few hours then dried on the rails in the boiler room.

After completion of exercises we returned to Hong Kong where the torpedoes were transferred to the mother ship, HMS MEDWAY, for overhauling and re-charging.

When it was my turn to go ashore again (little wonder I never had any money) I went to Hong Kong race course, called Happy Valley, where most of the Chinese punters looked anything but happy. Only the Chinese bookmakers seemed to be pleased with their lot. I then visited the Peak Railway, consisting of two lines on which were two carriages, one counter balancing the other, and the whole pulled up and down by wire ropes operated by a winch. At the top was the Peak Hotel, from which was a marvellous view across to Kowloon and mainland China. Below was the cemetery and about a mile inland a large liner. It had been lifted up there by a tidal wave during a typhoon and was being dismantled bit by bit by

Chinese coolies, thereby giving employment to a fortunate few among countless thousands of the not so fortunate.

A few days later it started to blow up and we were informed another typhoon was imminent. In cases like this all sea-worthy vessels put to sea where they would ride out the storm. As WESTCOTT left harbour the crew battened down and all boats were secured. Everything that moved on the upper deck and in the mess decks was well anchored and life lines rigged. The ship soon had a heavy roll on and was taking it in green. Things got worse, the wind howled, and speech was impossible. Nobody was allowed on the upper deck. The ship moved slow ahead into the storm. The sea had reached terrific heights and this continued all day.

It was rough as the typhoon moved away, but we were at last able to get a hot drink and a meal. The ship's cat, which had run up the mast to the crow's nest, finally allowed itself to be rescued. It was scared out of its wits, but, after a drink of tinned milk and a tin of sardines, it carried on as though nothing had happened. Slowly we made our way back to Hong Kong to see the devastation there. TAMAR had been put in the centre of the basin, secured by ropes in all directions and was all right, but some sampans and junks that had been taking shelter near by had been smashed. Windows had been torn out of buildings and the landing piers damaged. Fortunately the storm was not as bad as it could have been and as far as I know no one was killed.

It was not long before we were back at sea again. This time we had only two submarines with us that fired two torpedoes each and within six hours we were heading back into harbour.

One day, while ashore I watched a craftsman in the back of a shop blowing glass. This led to make a point of studying some of the skills that were practised wherever space allowed. The skill of the Chinese was amazing and they enjoyed being watched. I saw shoes, embroidery, lace and many other things being made. The most interesting was to watch them work with ivory. It was so intriguing they couldn't get me out of the place. They were making statues of Buddha in all sizes. They carved small and large elephants. Some elephants were carved going over a bridge, large to small, all holding each others tails. It must have taken weeks to carve these works of art. I think the most beautiful pieces were ivory balls. They started with a solid piece of round ivory, which was carved in an intricate design. Another ball was then carved inside the first ball with the same intricate design. This was repeated four or five times, each time the balls getting smaller and smaller and all one inside the other. The craftsman I was watching had been working on this same brilliant piece of workmanship for weeks. The cost on completion of these masterpieces was way beyond my pocket, even though their wages was just a pittance. At least I had seen them made with my own eyes.

Walking down the main street on another occasion, my oppo and myself, out of curiosity, went into a tea shop, sometimes termed a Joss House. Inside, were cubicles which seated four people. We sat in one with a Chinese gentleman. We were each given a cup without a handle - more like a small basin. A waiter came around putting a teaspoonful of dark green Chinese tea in the cups. Another waiter came with a kettle of boiling water to fill them up. After letting it brew you drank it and, as soon as you had finished, the cup was filled with hot water again, using the same tea leaves. This was repeated three or four times. It seemed it only started to get weaker after the third cup. Of course there was no milk or sugar in the tea. That, of course, would have been sacrilege to a Chinese. Tea drinking was a serious affair with them. (Carry on like this and my eyes will start slanting.)

While drinking our tea we talked to the Chinese gentleman sitting in the same cubicle as us about the lovely thing we'd seen being made in the workshops. He could speak quite good English and appeared to be well educated. I asked why in the Middle East, India and China, the cradle of the civilised world that had accumulated knowledge and skills for thousands of years, so much poverty and sub-standard squalor was evident on all sides. He said he could not speak for the Middle East of India but in the days of the powerful Chinese Mandarins, craftsmen who were old and infirm and no longer quick and agile at their trade were either executed or thrown on to the streets. Consequently, and in order to avoid this fate, when they taught apprentices they always kept some of their skills back, which in turn made them indispensable. As the craftsmen died, so that little bit of knowledge died with them and the country became poorer. In the end, the craft died out and was lost. However, they were beginning to build it up again. Another reason for the decline, I believe, was the increase in the population and gambling. They gambled incessantly - at the race course, at cards and mah jong. They played pitch and toss on the pavements and it seemed to me they gambled every cent they had, everyone trying to make a quick fortune. No work was done and the majority of them progressively grew poorer and poorer, and so became victims of their own folly. But at least they were still making things of beauty.

On coming out of the tea shop we decided on a rickshaw race so got one each back to the ship. It was a great experience. The poor coolies pulled like mad, knowing a further dollar was the reward to the winner, but as I was by far the lighter in weight it was my man that hit the front and stayed there until we reached the dockyard gates.

The Chinese Theatre was a memorable experience even though I could not understand a word of the language. It was easy to follow and get the gist of the plot as it was all in mime. The dancing was lovely and the use of the hands for expression was so impressive. The finger nails of the girls were about two inches long. Their skill with the fans and their glorious costumes were a fantastic sight to see. The music was different, but the musicians were very good and, although strange, it all proved enjoyable and well worth seeing.

On my next trip ashore I continued exploring and went across the water by ferry to Kowloon. Kowloon was not as busy as Hong Kong, but there was still plenty to see. On taking a long walk to the border of China I went quite a distance before the Customs Post eventually loomed up, manned by the Army, who kindly obliged with a bottle of cold Tiger Beer. It also transpired that one of the soldiers came from England on HMT ETTRICK at the same time as myself. All too soon it was time to retrace my steps, return to Kowloon and take the ferry to Hong Kong.

On the other side I ran into a Chinese funeral making its way along the main street. In front of the cortege the mourners were setting off fireworks, running round the bier and throwing them as they went. It was supposed to ward off evil spirits. The coffin was on top of a flowered, three-deck bier. It looked beautiful, the whole being supported by twelve Chinese, six down either side, holding long bamboo poles which were secured to a platform covered in silk. There was a five piece band playing and everyone was dressed in glorious coloured clothing. It looked like a wedding instead of a funeral. It must have been quite an influential person, as the higher the deceased was on the bier, the more important the person had to be.

The temperature was now rising well into the nineties. It was a job trying to keep cool. On board WESTCOTT there were no showers or baths. All we had was a bucket. This was filled with water, with one or two drops of Lysol disinfectant. If not too careful and some went into the eyes they'd be sore for a week. With eyes tightly shut you then tipped the bucket over your head followed by a bucket of clean water. The clean cold water was a welcome relief from the heat of the day. Cinemas being air conditioned, they were often the best place to visit in order to keep cool, but not always as entertaining as the theatre. Of course, another place to keep cool was the sea, but one had to be careful in choosing where to swim.

As in most naval bases at home and abroad there were quite a lot of R.N. personnel that were shore-based in Hong Kong. It was a great job for them. Some had their own flats and went home in the evening as if returning from work in civilian life. They paid a girl to clean the flat, cook meals, and go out with them. The only restriction was, if they did go out with the Chinese girl, she had to walk behind him, not with him, as was the custom in that part of the world. Some of these lads, especially the petty and chief petty officers, had it so good, that after serving a two and a half year commission with the thought of returning to Blighty looming up, there was a great wailing and gnashing of teeth and devious means employed to stay on for a further commission.

It was now July and we were off to sea again, this time to Wei Hai Wei. Travelling up the coast of China, it looked very barren. Vegetation was dead, just like the colour of sand, until we reached Wei Hai Wei. Here trees grew and everything looked cool and green, just like home. I believe years ago the British planted a variety of trees and shrubs here. They certainly improved the appearance of this island.

Having anchored half a mile inshore, along with the rest of the China Fleet, all the ships had their sides and superstructures cleaned and painted. Soon the Fleet looked ready for a royal review. Ashore there was very little to do except walk through the wooded glades, as there were only a few houses, Deh Sheng's general store, and some tea rooms.

Nobody was allowed ashore before nine in the morning and had to be back on board by nine o'clock at night. Apparently there was an agreement with the Japanese that between nine in the evening and nine in the morning the Japanese took over the island. In other words they had the night shift. Each night you would hear the chug chug boat, as they called it. It was a little diesel tug and on board there were about ten Japanese. They came from the mainland of China and religiously took charge for twelve hours.

A regatta was arranged between all our ships. The whalers were lowered, one being used for rowing and the other for sailing. I was put in the sailing crew. Different crews were timed until each ship picked the best crew they could muster. A course was laid out with marker buoys and the regatta started on the Saturday after we'd been there a week. There was a crew of five on the whalers, one officer and four of the best oarsmen the ship could muster. The course was a mile long and when the race commenced the whalers were followed by the skimmers and motor boats, all crammed with officers with loud hailing equipment, encouraging their own crews along. The race was then re-run with double crews. This was hilarious as the oarsmen were crammed in like sardines. Everybody on WESTCOTT got where they could see the best, watching the races from the bridge, on top of the guns, any place that was high up, cheering their heads off in support of our own crews. It was great! Next it was the turn of the cutters from the big ships. They had a crew of nine. Here again they were cheered on their way. Everyone was having a good time. Then it was our turn in the sailing competition. As it happened, I wasn't picked. The boats sailed round the anchored fleet finishing at the Admiral's flagship. We only came fifth but it didn't matter, just taking part was enough. The cutter's sailing crews were next. The roars from the big ships could be heard all round the Fleet. When the regatta was over the ships of the Fleet sailed past the flagship and the admiral took the salute. After we had come to rest again, a signal was hauled to the mast head of the flagship. "Splice the Main Brace!", and we all got an extra tot of rum.

The next day was a day of rest. As always when in harbour on Sunday morning, Divisions were held on the quarter deck. Then the skipper did his rounds inspecting the messes and all parts of the ship. In the afternoon I went ashore and after a walk round the island went swimming, and at four o'clock the motor boat came to pick us up to take us back to the ship in time for tea.

While there three Chinese nuns were given permission to come on board with hand-made kimonos. They were in green, red, blue, black and white - the kimonos that is, not the nuns! Down the back was a magnificent golden dragon and two smaller ones at the front. All were hand sewn and embroidered. They must have taken ages to make and this was reflected in the price, which I most certainly could not afford, but they were certainly worth every penny being asked, although I really couldn't see who would wear them. Certainly too rich and expensive-looking and I suppose they might best be seen in a museum - certainly a bit over the top for a run-ashore back in Darlington.

The following day our skipper, who was a physical fitness enthusiast, decided we would all compete in a run round the island. I didn't really want to go as I had already walked round it and knew what it looked like. However, no excuses would be taken and I had to join the happy throng. Some who had learnt earlier what the skipper had in store for us commenced to jog up and down to get themselves as fit as possible for the great day. When it arrived, about thirty or more of us lined up and the coxswain started us off.

I plodded on as best as I could, way behind the experts. Then, I started passing some of them. The first had twisted his ankle, the next had pulled a muscle and another had cramp. I stopped, had a rest and a chat with the casualties, and then carried on to the finish, coming in about twentieth. Before returning to the ship we all had a swim to cool off. There was no doubt, taking everything into consideration, we were having a fine time. I believe the winners of this race had to race against those off other ships, so half the British Fleet must have done a fair old bit of running around Wei Hai Wei in those days.

It was not long after the final race before the Fleet started to disperse, some to Shanghai, some to Hong Kong and others to Singapore. We were nearly the last to leave and just before we left, a Japanese cruiser came into the anchorage. Out came the binoculars to have a look at her, but the crafty devils had covered up all their guns and torpedo tubes. I think they had come to look at our Fleet but most of our ships had gone by then. Goodness knows what they thought of WESTCOTT - guns missing, no torpedo tubes. A sad state of affairs, they must have decided.

Because we were Commander S we had a doctor on board. While at Wei Hai Wei I developed ear trouble which the doctor could not cure, so on arriving at Hong Kong I was transferred to HMS MEDWAY, where I was kept for two weeks. During my time on board I discovered what a marvellous ship she was. On one deck was a complete workshop with lathes, drills, grinders and saws. Here they overhauled the torpedoes the submarines had fired, stripping them down and re-charging them with air and fuel.

The messes were roomy and plenty of them. About six messes were reserved for the submarine crews, who certainly deserved a rest from the cramped conditions they were subjected to on the 'boats'. After two weeks my ear infection improved - although only a temporary cure - and I was discharged. By this time WESTCOTT had sailed away, although where to I hadn't the faintest idea. However I was put on board HMS CORNWALL, a county class cruiser, which must have been going to where my old ship was. Again I was to sample life aboard a big ship and it was great. Soon CORNWALL left Hong Kong bound for Singapore where I found WESTCOTT. War clouds were in the air and everyone was talking about it, so I expected my ship would be having her torpedoes and gun replaced. On arrival, there in harbour was D47 looking just the same as I had left her and I was quickly transferred. I cannot say whether I was happy or sad about it. From a big roomy ship to a small cramped one was not too appealing. Nevertheless, here I was back with my mates again.

Looking around the dockyard it seemed it wasn't any different to any other, except here they had the largest dry dock in the Far East. There was also a gigantic floating dock. The workers all seemed to be Chinese or Malay supervised by the British, a noble roll for ex-British dockyard workers.

When the opportunity arrived I went ashore to get my first glimpse of Singapore. The first thing I noticed was an open air cinema and a swimming pool in the dockyard. The pool, of course, was out of bounds to me because of my ear. Going further afield I ventured into the town. Of all the places in the Far East, Singapore was the nicest. The streets were wide and clean, the shops were better and the shopkeepers were not begging you to buy all the time. One thing you had to be careful of was huge open culverts that ran down the main streets. These were about five feet wide, five feet deep and semi-circular. When it rained the volume of water that passed down these drains was colossal.

One day out walking, I came across the famous Raffles Club. There was a commissionaire outside opening the doors for guests, who then walked under a colonnade on a red carpet into the foyer of the hotel. There must have been something special on. Inside I could see them drinking their cocktails, having tiffin, and living just as we didn't!

One evening I went to the open air cinema in the dockyard. It seemed strange sitting out in the open watching pictures. Every now and then a lizard crawled across the screen. Attendants on either side of the screen had long bamboo poles and would use these to knock the lizards off. It was funny to see a lizard crawling across Katherine Hepburn's face. Before the picture started and during the interval they came around with ice cream, nuts and a fruit called a pomelo. These were a cross between pomegranates and oranges. They peeled and split open like an orange, tasted like a pomegranate, and were delicious.

My ears were still causing trouble, so I was sent to Singapore General Hospital, where I had a mastoid operation and was a guest of theirs for seven weeks.

On 3rd September 1939 at six p.m. Singapore time, while listening to the radio we heard the declaration of war against

Germany announced. I thought of the last Great War and remembered what we were told during our training; we were paid to kill or be killed and nothing could be done about it other than to obey orders without question.

After about three weeks hospitalisation I was getting on fine, and accepted the offer when a lady came to the hospital and asked if anybody would like a ride in her car, so I said yes. Once permission was obtained from the ward sister, I was taken for a look around Singapore. She certainly knew the place better than I ever could.

We first went to the Singapore Swimming Club, in town. Inside were two open air pools. The smaller for children with slides and various playthings. The main pool was much bigger and had high diving boards, spring boards and another slide. It looked so inviting. Around the pool people sat at tables, under umbrellas, drinking. Waiters in white were dashing about between the tables, taking orders and serving. Everyone was in bathing costumes. At the far end was a clubhouse which, because of the heat, was not being used. It looked really elegant inside.

My escort sat me down at a table and bought me a drink. She spoke to one or two people she knew, probably explaining why I was there. After leaving the club we drove through town to the park. Monkeys were everywhere. Nuts were being sold to feed them, hence so many, so we joined in with the other visitors and fed the monkeys.

Leaving the park we drove out into the country where we passed a huge mansion belonging to the wealthy Tiger Balm family. It was a magnificent building. I was told they had places like this all over the Far East. Their business was in manufacturing ointment, known as balm, and I believe they were also in the brewing business, Tiger Beer. After a most refreshing day out we returned to the hospital where I thanked my escort and said goodbye to a very kind lady.

Ex-Officers of HMS Westcott
From Left to Right:
Noel Britten : S Farquharson Roberts : Ernest Quarrie
Brian De Courcey-Ireland : Michael Wilson
Trevor Riches : Bill Loughborough (Doc)

CHAPTER FIVE

Westward Ho!

Leaving hospital after seven weeks I returned to WESTCOTT and found much had been transformed since I was last on board. The winch on Y platform had been removed, and Y gun was replaced. The derrick between the two torpedo racks had gone and also the racks. In their place were the original torpedo tubes. Just for'ad of the wardroom flat had been fitted two depth-charge throwers, one on either side, and two depth-charge release-racks had been welded into position on the stern. Finally, the searchlight had been replaced between two sets of torpedo tubes.

The following day it had been arranged to munition ship. They must have been waiting for my return. The whole ship's company had to take part. No one was excused, including officers and torpedoemen with bad ears. The magazine and shell rooms were opened up, fore and aft. When the munitions train arrived, cordite, shells and detonators were passed from hand to hand and put in their respective places. Hundreds of shells, all different kinds - star, high explosive and armour-piecing - went into different marked racks, and the cordite into the magazines.

At one hundred and ten degrees in the shade it was no joke. Perspiration poured from us. We were given salt tablets to suck, helping to replace the salt lost from the body due to perspiration. Once completed, each watch took it in turn to cool off in the dockyard pool. In my case I had to be content with buckets of water over myself, with my ears stuffed with cotton wool. They certainly needed to be protected against a repeat performance of what had just put me in hospital.

The next day thirty depth charges were loaded into their respective places, nine into each release rack and two in the throwers. The remainder were stowed either side of the after superstructure. We were now able to fire a pattern of five depth charges at any one time. Each charge contained three hundred pounds of TNT or amatol. When this job was completed we took aboard six 21" torpedoes and fitted their warheads with the assistance of the dockyard crane. The torpedoes weighed well over a ton and the heads were five hundred pounds each.

After the heavy work had been completed we torpedoemen fitted the pistols (the firing mechanism) in the depth charges. With the detonators in place, we screwed them into the main charge and fitting the primers into the other end had the job completed.

The same procedure was done with the pistols of the torpedoes, only a little propeller on the pistol drove the detonator into the primer as the torpedo went through the water. Smoke floats were fastened on top of the depth charge racks.

On the third day we went to sea. The range finder and all the guns were lined up and tested. Searchlight carbons were adjusted and the iris shutter oiled and tested. At last we were beginning to look like a real destroyer; albeit rather an old one.

Back in harbour, twenty four additions to the crew awaited us, including eight torpedoemen. The ship now had a complement of one hundred and thirty four; Our mess had eleven torpedoemen plus seven new seamen. The other messes were also increased in number and each now contained eighteen men.

The new seamen were all conscripts, called HO's. (Hostilities Only). They had each experienced only six weeks basic training to date so had a lot to learn about a sailor's life aboard a man of war. It was with this crew I was to spend my next two and a half years.

Our Chinese mess boys were given a chance to stay with the ship until we left Singapore or to be taken back to Hong Kong on the next available ship. They all elected to go home. The poor lads would now be out of work, but knowing how good they were, I bet a lot came to Britain after the war and started up the first Chinese take-aways!

We now had to cater for ourselves, so one of the lads in our mess elected to give it a try. He only lasted three months, so I took over, retaining the job until I left the ship more than two years later. The Chinese women who came aboard to take away our washing, returning it white and clean, were fast becoming a thing of the past too. It was not long before we were all doing our own dhobying. Life was getting tougher by the minute.

While in harbour the ship's company had to practice boat drill, gun drill, torpedo and depth charge drill. Action stations were sprung all times of the day and night. We were learning fast there was a real war on now and survival was to depend on just how well and how rapidly we could cope with its reality.

One day a stoker brought a monkey on board. It became the terror of the ship. He kept it by the break of the fo'c's'le. Anybody walking out of the mess on to the iron deck it would lean over the fo'c's'le and pinch his hat, if it could. It was impossible to get a hat back. The more he was chased, the more the monkey liked it. Up the mast it would scamper, and by the time it had finished there was nothing left of the hat.

The ship's cat hated it too and kept its distance. Most of us remembered to keep out of its way and kept to the other side of the ship. Complaining to the owner only got a laugh, but little did he know the monkey's days were numbered as it fortuitously disappeared at sea one fine day, to everyone's relief, except possibly the owner's.

We went to sea and arrived off the coast of Burma. What for, nobody knew until a signalman said we were looking for a German merchant ship, SCHARNHORST, making her way along the coast from Japan to Germany. At dawn a merchant ship was sighted but she didn't tally with the description we had of her. She was flying the flag of Panama so, after a brief signal, we let her go. Later it transpired they were changing her appearance by adding an extra funnel or altering the shape of the superstructure as well as flying the flags of different nations. Every credit should go to her Captain for his initiative and ingenuity in which he managed to alter the ship whereby she was able to avoid capture and reach Germany.

Back in Singapore we took on board an expert diver with all his equipment, and left for Sarawak, off the coast of Borneo. On arrival we anchored about a mile off shore and lowered the motor boat, into which was transferred the diver, his diving equipment and a manually operated pump. Four of us, were detailed to see to all his needs, and the boat was taken to a buoy and tied to it.

The diver then donned all his regalia - a clumsy suit, big iron boots, a steel helmet along with heavy lead weights fastened to his chest and back. Once his air line, lowering rope, signal line and face plate were correctly fitted, he was lowered into the water. We then started slowly to turn the handle of the pump which supplied him with air, taking it in turns to operate the pump and tend his lines, half an hour at a time, hour after hour.

The object of the exercise was to put explosive charges under the oil lines, which ran from the oil tanks ashore, to buoys about a mile out to sea indicating the re-fuelling terminals to which ships would connect. The cables connected to the explosives were led to a building on shore, where they would be detonated if and when considered necessary.

With the motor boat rocking all over the place, the stench of petrol and sea water plashing about the bottom of the boat, we were all feeling pretty squeamish by the time we got back to WESTCOTT. I am pleased to say we four only did it for one day as somebody else took the job over until completed.

Meanwhile the rest of the crew were diving into the warm sea, swimming, having a great time and keeping cool into the bargain. Marksmen stood by with rifles to repel sharks. Fortunately none were seen, so all was fine. After three days the job was completed and we returned to harbour.

On reaching Singapore WESTCOTT commenced taking on oil fuel ready for our next voyage. The method used was through a manhole situated in our mess. This was lifted and a large four-inch diameter armoured hose was led from the upper deck through our mess and the oil then pumped into a tank under the stoker's mess. It was the stokers' responsibility to take care of this and after the pipe was in place, a relay of stokers shouted instructions to start and stop the pumping as required.

I was in our mess when the stoker's shout, "Stop pumping!" was repeated along the line, but the pumping did not stop. When the oil started to overflow into our mess I dashed to my locker and managed to remove most of my clothes from it but oil got to the outside of my kit bag, my duck suit, which I never used, and a few books. These I threw away, with the exception of my Bible, which still has its tell-tale stains to this day.

Those who weren't present to salvage their gear were compensated with new clothes. I was given a new kit bag when one became available. As far as the duck suit was concerned, we had stopped using these Number Five suits ages ago, so I never bothered to claim. It was one piece of luggage less to carry about.

After this fiasco the great clean up started. We all set to with buckets, cloths and cotton waste. It took what seemed an eternity to clean up the oil and far longer to get rid of the smell. There were no modern detergents in those days so paraffin was used and then a good scrub with hot soapy water. The air was blue - and not just from the fumes of the oil or paraffin.

The war, so far, had not had any real effect on us. Life was more or less normal, more so for people ashore. From the news received from home it seemed to be the same there. I believe they were calling it the phoney war in the newspapers.

On board we were sweltering in heat. When we laid down, even in the shade, the imprints of our bodies was to be seen in perspiration on the surface of where we'd been lying. Those going ashore would decide on visiting cinemas irrespective of what film was showing because the cinemas were all cool and air conditioned. Occasionally, there were cooling monsoons but these ferocious storms only lasted a short time and within an hour it would be just as hot and dry as before.

During our stay in Sarawak we ran short of food, so somebody decided to buy a live piglet once back to Singapore. That way we would never go hungry again - a noble thought. In order to accommodate this little pig, the wash down locker under the whaler was cleared and brooms, etc. removed to the starboard one. The lockers were perforated allowing the water to run away which was ideal for the pig. Straw was placed in the bottom, and the lid lifted during the hours of daylight. To exercise the pig each day a rope was placed round its neck, it was lifted out and then walked up and down the iron deck by its owner. While he was doing this somebody else would be cleaning the locker out. Food was provided by each mess donating their left-overs and potato peelings, which were washed and boiled. The pig was growing nicely.

On January 28th 1940 WESTCOTT left the China Station. It would be the last time I would see Singapore, although I did not know it at the time. Our job was to escort a large floating dock being towed back to England by sea-going tugs. At eight bells we were on our way doing about three knots. Fortunately the sea was calm and the towing going to plan. After a few days we had to leave the floating dock. It was now safely on its long journey home. We then proceeded to Colombo.

While on our way there, during the morning watch, a school of flying fish was seen heading straight for the ship. Instead of trying to avoid us they swam right into the side of the ship and those dropping on the deck made a fine breakfast for those who collected and took them up the galley.

The pig had been on board for over two months now and we had been feeding it well. It was nearly twice as big as when brought aboard. Getting too large to keep any longer, the skipper told the owner it must go. The argument then arose as to who should kill it. The owner said it was his pet, he couldn't do it. No one else seemed inclined. That is, all except Tanky. He said he had been a butcher in civilian life so he would kill it. We all thought, under the circumstances, it would be best to leave it to the expert.

Out came his sharp knives, plus a piece of wood about four inches square and three feet long. He then drove a six inch nail right through one end of it until the point was protruding two inches. Then he obtained the petty officers' tin bath and filled it with boiling water, with a steam line in to keep it hot. When all was ready we rushed for the most advantageous position to witness this spectacle. I was on the fo'c's'le looking down.

Two of the lads were told by Tanky to hold the pig's legs tight, when he hit it to stun it. Then he would hang it up, cut it's throat and put it into the bath, so that the hairs on it's skin would come off easily. That was the theory. When all was ready, Tanky brought down the wood with all his might, but missed. In their eagerness to assist, the two matelots lifted the pig up, but then accidentally dropped it into the bath of very hot water.

The pig, squealing like mad, jumped out of the bath and raced down the starboard side of the ship, towards the after superstructure. It turned, then commenced running down the port side towards the break of the fo'c's'le where Tanky was waiting for it with his piece of wood with the nail in. The pig saw him. Turning back it ran towards the owner who was holding his arms out wide in order to catch it. The pig must have lost every confidence in all its erstwhile friends by this time because it quickly turned again; but this time it slipped, slid under the guard rail and finished up in the ocean: where at least it must have met a more merciful death.

What with the pig squealing and matelots screaming and shouting advice, most of us were hysterical with laughter. It was certainly hilarious, but we lost a good dinner.

Arriving at Colombo we fuelled and re-provisioned, then proceed to Aden with the County Class Cruiser, HMS DORSETSHIRE. While running parallel with her she noticed our ship's side was dirty and sent a signal to that effect. So, in order to please her Commanding Officer, we had two men hanging precariously on staging over the side while the ship was doing fifteen knots. The two doing the job and the two in attendance were not pleased at all. It was extremely dangerous and I wondered what the official reaction would have been if one of them had fallen or been washed off.

Continuing to Aden and the Red Sea we met up with the battle-cruiser HMS HOOD along with six liners filled with Australian and New Zealand troops. If I remember rightly the liners were QUEEN ELIZABETH, QUEEN MARY, EMPRESS OF INDIA, EMPRESS OF CANADA, EMPRESS OF BRITAIN and MAURITANIA. The battle-cruiser HOOD looked like a pinnace alongside these huge ships. So, there we were, HOOD in the lead with the six liners in three pairs behind and three destroyers down either flank. Further out of sight were two county class cruisers, HMS CORNWALL to port and HMS DORSETSHIRE to starboard, with the aircraft carrier HMS EAGLE astern; our first of many convoys.

With the ship's side clean and the staging stowed away, our speed was increased to twenty eight knots. The sea was now rushing and roaring past. If the side had been left alone the sea would have cleaned it for us. Our poor ship was belching out smoke from the funnel as if there was no tomorrow. The skipper was going mad. The engineers tried hard to stop it, which they eventually achieved after a nasty signal this time from the mighty HOOD - but these great ships were going too fast for poor old WESTCOTT. Being sadly in need of a boiler clean didn't help. Finally the convoy had to settle down to the speed of the slowest ship, which happened to be ours.

On we raced past Aden into the Red Sea and on to Port Suez. Here the aircraft carrier and the two cruisers left us. HOOD and the three destroyers went through the canal first, the liners coming up behind. The last of the destroyers was HMS

WESTCOTT. By the time we reached Port Said they had all gone speeding off on their way to Britain and WESTCOTT was left to make its own way as best it could.

We headed for Malta, arriving on February 14th 1940. Here Commander Corrie-Hill left the ship and the new Captain, Lieutenant Commander Seagrave, took over. We were sorry to see Commander Corrie-Hill go and, piping the side, said goodbye to him and welcomed our new Captain aboard.

While in Malta we were attached to HMS GLORIOUS and in April, together with HMS ARK ROYAL and HMS BULLDOG, left the Mediterranean to join the Home Fleet - BULLDOG and WESTCOTT providing anti-submarine protection.

Just before we left it was found one of our challenge lights on the port yard arm was out. These lights were at the very end of the yard arm and I was detailed to go aloft to replace it. Armed with a screw driver, a pair of pliers and a lamp, up the mast I went. Reaching the yard arm I gingerly edged my way long with my feet in the rope stirrups, with one hand 'working for the king' and the other, clinging to the yard, for myself. Replacing the offending lamp I clawed my way back along the yardarm and down the mast, all the time hoping fervently that I would never ever have to do it again. When watching those young sailors doing their antics up the mast at the Edinburgh Tattoo I wonder where they get the nerve from. Fortunately all ships had hand-held sets of challenge lights. These were normally used as they could be tested quickly before use, so the need for those on the yard arm was extremely remote.

Our watch-keeping system was changed from four to three - red, white and blue - on the way to the more perilous home waters. During my time on watch I sat with three others on the quarter deck keeping lookout and ready to fire the depth charges if so instructed. Here, for days on end, we watched the wake of the ship as we sped along with one pair of binoculars between us, with which we'd take it in turn to keep lookout while the others unfolded the story of their lives to each other.

Without modern sound reproduction on the messdeck for entertainment purposes our only music came via a little wind-up gramophone and records which could only be played when the seas were calm enough. There was also a radio but it crackled so much it was not worth listening to.

A lot of my time was taken up devising meals. For breakfast it was just bread and jam or marmalade. For dinner there were stews, pies, Cornish pasties and, on Sundays, a roast of something, if we had anything. I made pastry myself and eventually got quite good at it. They all ate it, anyway. For tea we had bully beef, pilchards, or some other tinned stuff such as Spam. Supper was just anything that could be found on the mess shelves. Each day two of the lads were detailed for mess duties. They washed-up, scrubbed the tables, and the forms and lockers on which we sat.

Every Sunday was like a spring clean. About four men off each mess set to cleaning and washing, then polishing everything in sight, until everywhere was spick and span. All then dressed in their best uniform (No.1s) and at eleven o'clock the skipper did his rounds. If the skipper was busy then Jimmy the One took his place, inspecting everything.

After rounds we went to church service on the quarter deck. Afterwards, if we were not on duty watch, the time was our own. In harbour we usually went ashore but if at sea we spent our time stretched out in the sun or pacing up and down the deck, a usual practice to keep bodily fitter while on board.

The 17th March 1940 was my twenty-first birthday whereby I qualified for my first good conduct badge. This indicated three years of sterling service and carried with it an additional threepence (old money) per day. Thinking that at this rate I'd soon be in the surtax class I made a mental note that once back in England I'd look around for some kind of investment into which I could pour this new flood of wealth. Maybe a row of houses in the posh part of Darlington!

During dinner the lads each gave me a sip of their tot and by one o'clock I was out cold. Too drunk to get in my hammock I was laid on the lockers, where I slept until the following morning - nearly twenty-four hours. How they managed without me I will never know.

On our way to Plymouth it was decided we should go into two watches - very tiring indeed. All sleep and watch-keeping and little time for the jobs that needed doing around the ship.

On April 19th WESTCOTT arrived at Devonport - fifteen months after I had set off from Southampton aboard HMT ETTRICK - for a long-overdue boiler clean. Starboard watch was given four days leave, subject to recall at any time. When starboard watch returned from leave it was our turn, so off I went. It was nice to see all the folks at home again, but time was very short. It took me twenty-four hours to get there and back, so I didn't have much time to do the socialising I'd like to have done.

Boiler cleaning was over by the time my leave was up and I returned aboard as dockyard electricians were running degaussing cables round the ship to de-magnetise it, a safeguard against magnetic mines. They were also fitting acoustic gear to protect the ship against mines that were triggered by sound. The acoustic gear sent sound waves ahead of the ship in order to blow up the mines before we reached them. (We hoped!)

Before going back to sea, our cap tallies were taken away and replaced with others with just H.M.S. - a security measure. All this was done in just over a week. On completion we were ready to get back to war.

CHAPTER SIX

Back in Home Waters.

Leaving Devonport, WESTCOTT headed up the English Channel towards the cold North Sea. The skipper decided to keep us in two watches, much to the despair of the ship's company; watch and watch is so very tiring.

Proceeding north we passed familiar places like Whitby, Redcar and Newcastle. Familiar to me, that is, as we were just about thirty miles from my home. Keeping on north, past Scotland and the Shetlands, we proceeded into the cold, grey waters of the Atlantic. On we went at about twenty knots until Norway's bleak and forbidding mountains reaching right down to the sea, hove into view. Arriving at Narvik, we were greeted by the gruesome sight of the damaged Tribal Class destroyer HMS ESKIMO.

She was patrolling just outside the fjord, continually going astern, because her bows had been blown off. I can imagine the relief when they saw us appear to take over her arduous task. She would soon be steaming her long way back home in this strange way for the repairs she so urgently needed. The damage was the result of a torpedo attack during the second battle of Narvik. Sadly ESKIMO lost eighteen men when the torpedo struck.

It is worth recalling the Battle of Narvik, although WESTCOTT wasn't present. Ten German destroyers, each carrying two hundred soldiers, landed there to secure a beach-head. Together with air support they began systematically to harass our forces ashore. The Germans were smug in the belief that all was well. However, unknown to them, one of our aircraft spotted their ships. So while they were asleep, at four in the morning, on April 10th 1940, five British destroyers led by HMS HARDY, went into the fjord, sank two German destroyers, and damaged two more.

During this engagement we lost HMS HUNTER and HARDY was beached because of severe damage. HMS HOTSPUR was hit, HMS HAVOC and HMS HOSTILE were unscathed and along with HOTSPUR withdrew, bringing with them the survivors off the other two ships. During this engagement, unfortunately Captain D was killed.

A short time later the Second Battle of Narvik took place, when the battleship HMS WARSPITE and nine destroyers, HMS BEDOUIN, COSSACK, PUNJABI, ESKIMO, ICARUS, KIMBERLY, HERO, FORESTER and FOXHOUND, went in to engage the remainder of the German destroyers. However, this time the enemy was prepared. Although the German destroyers were nearly twice the size of ours and could be classed as light cruisers the odds were in our favour for a change. The outcome was a foregone conclusion..

During this engagement HMS ESKIMO was torpedoed, but it was gratifying to know that all the German ships were sunk. It was a great naval victory and a serious blow to the German Navy. It must have been disheartening for the German soldiers watching their ships being sunk one by one, plus one of their U-boats sunk by our aircraft.

It was a pity the victory at sea was not matched by similar successes on shore, but it was not to be. The victorious

German Army, along with their air power, overwhelmed our forces; and our army, encamped precariously by the water's edge, was under constant attack from the air as well as from the German soldiers on the cliffs above them.

After patrolling outside Narvik Fjord for a time we were directed to Andenes to evacuate our soldiers there. At the same time our troops were also being evacuated from Dunkirk. Things were looking black for us - the war was certainly not going our way.

At Andenes as many men as possible were ferried on board using our motorboat and whalers. As the soldiers waded their way out to reach our boats, they threw their rifles into the water in disgust. Luckily, the machine-guns were kept.

When we couldn't get any more men on board WESTCOTT started out for Britain, while other ships took our place to complete the evacuation. Heading out of the fjord a Junkers 88 and 87 arrived on the scene and commenced attacking us. The situation was farcical as well as critical. Our main armament could not elevate high enough to be of any use, so the only defence we had was our single-barrel pom-pom, which jammed after firing half a dozen rounds. There we were, helpless, with all these soldiers on board.

The army lads, seeing our predicament, mounted their machine guns in the best places available, and helped give some indication that we were a fighting ship. At the same time, we had an Aldis lamp on the pom-pom platform which was flashed towards the aircraft in time with a drumbeat on the bottom of a mess kettle. My God, what a way to fight a war. It might well have been a forerunner to a Dad's Army episode.

Fortunately, more by good luck than good management, we escaped safely into the Atlantic, making our way quickly to Scapa Flow to disembark the troops. What those lads thought of us, the Lord knows. I presume the Germans thought we were one of their ships when they saw the flashing light and called off the attack; or maybe they had just run out of bombs. Whatever the reason that was a lucky break for WESTCOTT.

After disembarking the soldiers we took on fuel, re-provisioned, and then returned to Norway. This time we went to Trondheim to evacuate more soldiers. There were no more incidents and we landed them back in Scotland safely before returning to Narvik.

On our way up the Norwegian coast the weather was much more favourable. For the first time I went on the middle watch with the sun shining. On completion of my four hours stint it was still shining. It only went dark between one and two o'clock in the morning. It was truly the land of the Midnight Sun. To crown the glory of it all was the flashing of the Northern Lights.

Reaching Narvik we went into the fjord, this time to help protect our remaining troops. A contingent of British soldiers were on the opposite side of the fjord to that of the Germans. It became necessary to walk up the port side of the ship going up the fjord and the starboard side on the way down, because the Germans were sniping at us from the shore. While patrolling the fjord it was prudent to keep off the upper deck, only going there when changing watches. In any case, being in two watches, it was a matter of watch-keeping, eating and sleeping.

WESTCOTT continued patrolling inside the fjord for a few days, during which time our soldiers ashore and our ship were subjected to attacks from the air. Fortunately, the sides of the mountains were so steep that when the aircraft dropped their bombs the angle of descent missed us completely, as we manoeuvred under the shelter of the mountain sides. I'm sure the soldiers wished they could do the same.

On the German side of the fjord was a railway which ran through a tunnel. The Germans made use of this by bringing up a large gun mounted on a flat wagon. After firing a few rounds at us it would retreat into the tunnel. We fired back hoping to cause an avalanche, but it was to no avail, so, while keeping them at bay, we called up the battleship HMS WARSPITE, with its fifteen inch guns. On arrival it soon made short work of the railway and the gun.

It was apparent that our soldiers were getting nowhere fast so the adjutant ashore and the flag officer on board WARSPITE decided to embark the troops and we all retired from Narvik, saying farewell to the beached HARDY as we passed.

WESTCOTT was now running short of rations. Fresh meat had disappeared after four or five days. After nine or ten days we were cutting the mould off the bread and eating the inside. Corned beef, spam and tinned herrings along with hard tack, was all we had left, and we were grateful to have that. The two-watch system was sapping our energy also. Hammocks were constantly up and nobody wasted time on stripping off or washing before climbing into them when coming off a first or middle watch. Some forewent their 'mick' and just flung themselves on the lockers fully-booted-and-spurred.

Leaving Narvik we proceeded with WARSPITE to Harstad on the Lofoten Isle. Approaching Harstad the beautiful Aurora Borealis, or Northern Lights, could be seen. It seems the light from the sun caused a reflection from the ice caps of the North Pole which creates a flashing and continual movement effect in the sky. This spectacular natural exhibition was a sight that once seen can never be forgotten, but it is doubtful whether many of us at the time were able to appreciate it. To appreciate such natural beauty one needed time, ease and a sense of well-being. A state of mind more in keeping with Wordsworth contemplating his daffodils than a bunch of war weary young sailors contemplating the luxury of a deep sleep.

On entering Harstad harbour we tied up alongside a county class cruiser, HMS KENT, from which we took on fuel and a few supplies. The following day more troops embarked aboard KENT and other big ships. This would be the final evacuation of Norway as far as the Royal Navy was concerned. Early in May, WESTCOTT formed part of the escort group for HMS ARK ROYAL, HMS KENT and HMS WARSPITE, escorting these big ships back to Scapa Flow. On arrival, WESTCOTT was dispatched to Dunfermline for minor repairs. Here we were granted shore leave and I was glad to get my feet on terra firma again. After an unsuccessful attempt at ice-skating at the local rink, a party of us made our way to Edinburgh where a fine time was had by all. The Scots made us very welcome no matter where we went. After a week the engine-room repairs were complete and WESTCOTT was ordered to join the 11th Destroyer Flotilla, Western Approaches Command. Once again we were destined for the cold waters of the North Atlantic. Arriving at our appointed rendezvous we met up with our first Atlantic convoy, consisting of thirty-five merchant ships and eight escorts. Picking up our station we commenced to zigzag all the way back to the UK.

The weather took a turn for the worse and we were getting drenched by sea spray whenever we went on watch. It became very cold. On my station, just outside the officers' galley, near the depth charges, were three other torpedoemen. All huddled together trying to keep warm, watching for anything that might threaten us at the same time. The convoy was travelling at about seven knots. It became a long slow plod for the trip itself was uneventful. Approaching land the merchant ships peeled off, some to Northern Ireland, others to Glasgow, Liverpool and Milford Haven. When the last merchant ship had left we proceed round Land's End to Devonport.

After taking on board fuel and provisions, we were sent out on a submarine chase with our sister ship, HMS WHIRLWIND. We travelled west, about ten miles apart, towards Lands End, sweeping the sea with our Asdics as we went. About 120 miles off Lands End WHIRLWIND was torpedoed. Racing to the scene we found her with her bows blown off. Oil was everywhere and men were walking around in a daze trying to tend the injured. The ship had lost all power and was floundering in the water. She was in a worse state than the ESKIMO at Narvik.

Going alongside we took off the survivors. Her skipper had been blown from the bridge to the deck below and his head was covered in bandages. It was obvious he was suffering from shock and did not know what he was doing. After searching for more men, we lay the dead on the deck of WHIRLWIND by the torpedo tubes and covered them with blankets. Twenty-nine had been killed. Twenty had gone with the bow of the ship and the remainder lay on her deck. Our skipper asked the skipper of WHIRLWIND what should be done with the wreck. They decided between them to sink it. So, standing off a thousand yards, we began to shell her. After firing about twenty rounds of 4" armour-piercing shells and only scoring two or three hits, it was decided to torpedo her. The gallant torpedo crew went to their stations and trained their tubes outboard. When the sights lined up, we fired and calmly awaited the big bang. Closely watching the wake of the torpedo we could see it was going to miss. Some said that the torpedo went round in a circle heading back towards us, but I never saw it.

What, with the gunnery and torpedo crews missing a standing target, each jeering the other, I was glad I was not involved; it was so pathetic. Again, the guns started firing, this time with more success, hitting WHIRLWIND and creating a fire on the after superstructure. It still would not go down. It was as if some mysterious hand was holding it up. Another torpedo was fired. After waiting for what seemed like ages HMS WHIRLWIND went up in a flash and down to the deep. Standing alongside me, by the torpedo tubes, was the chief stoker off WHIRLWIND. He was in tears. Part of his life was going beneath the waves - with maybe a friend or two laid out on her quarter deck.

Searching awhile for the U-boat and getting no Asdic contact we left, heading for Falmouth with the survivors. On our way back we asked what had happened. It seems they had got a contact on the U-boat and went into the attack. At the same time the U-boat fired a torpedo at them. The lad I was talking to said there was an almighty explosion and the next thing he saw was the bows of the ship going past him, slowly sinking as they went. He remembered seeing all the hammocks which were slung in the mess going down with her - a macabre sight. After disembarking the injured at Falmouth we returned to Devonport. The rest of the crew were sent to HMS DRAKE, the barracks for Devonport ratings.

After doing a couple of uneventful convoys during the month of August, quarter of the way to America and back, convoy OG40 and HG40 being the first, then OB201 and SC2 being the second, WESTCOTT was despatched to Devonport and from September to November underwent a refit, the crew being granted ten days leave each.

Starboard watch went first and while they were on leave, my mate and I went ashore to Plymouth with the leading steward with whom we had chummed up during our long hours watch-keeping on the quarter deck. After admiring Plymouth Hoe we started drinking Tia Marias and had a great night out. On returning to the ship we were invited down to the stewards' mess where out came a bottle of some unknown concoction which the leading steward had saved from nearly-empty bottles of wardroom tipple. After drinking this we were smashed to the eyeballs and vowed never to do it again - until the next time!

When I went ashore a day or two later, I exercised more discretion, going sight-seeing in Plymouth. On the front were the bowling greens of the famous Plymouth Hoe, a tourist attraction I suppose, as they were purported to have been in use since the great days of Sir Francis Drake.

When it was my turn to be duty watch on board and also because half the mess was on leave, I tried my hand at making Tiddy Oggies (cornish pasties) having tasted and enjoyed them during the wild run ashore with the leading steward. There were only a few in the mess and a little experimental catering might make it easier for the cook and myself - nothing ventured nothing gained! I prepared the potatoes, carrots, turnips, and onion, cutting them up small, then added the peas. While they were cooking I made the pastry. Rolling it flat, I cut out rings, using a plate as a template. I minced corned beef and, when the vegetables were cool, mixed them all together. Putting a portion onto each pastry ring. I folded them over and crimped the edges. Finally, I made a slot in the top to let out the steam. They were then ready to cook.

After making eighteen I gave them to the cook and told him to do his worst. They came out beautifully. Even the cook spoke well of the two he had. After that I was often asked to do it again, but could only do so when time allowed in harbour. At least they made me popular.

During our time there an able-seaman came on board who could speak and read German fluently. That gave us an interpreter who could listen to the U-boat commanders talking to each other when they were on the surface. The skipper would send for him whenever such transmissions were in progress. Whether he achieved any success with his efforts, I do not know.

Dockyard workers had started fitting emergency lighting. They looked like miner's lamps and were hung from the deck head. When the electrical supply was cut off these lights came on. It meant more work for me, testing circuits and charging the batteries, but they were very important as sudden darkness on board could create panic down in the bowels of the ship, especially when in action.

On return of the starboard watch it was our turn for leave, so, donning my No 1s off I went. On arriving in London things looked grim. The air-raids had started. At night people sheltered in the underground stations under the most appalling conditions. Women and children lay on the concrete platforms trying to sleep, while trains still pulled in and out of the stations.

It was difficult trying to find a pathway through the recumbent citizens without disturbing them. Catching my train to Darlington and passing slowly through North London I could see fires and devastation everywhere. How the people stood up to it I do not know - and this was only the beginning.

Arriving at my home town I found everything normal. Of course, rationing had started. Whatever you wanted cost coupons as well as money. It seemed coupons were more important than money. I stayed with my sister, gave her my coupons, and let her sort them out. It was grand to see all those friends and relations. After a lovely time, all too short, my leave came to an end, and soon I was surveying the tragic damage to London once again.

On returning to the ship we found it was time to start painting her. This time powers-that-be completely changed our colour to mauve. She looked awful, but we were stuck with it. This camouflage was supposed to give an extra few minutes of invisibility at dawn and dusk. If it saved us from the same fate as WHIRLWIND it would be worth it. Soon with our portholes closed and the dead-lights down, we were on our way, but not before a short length of rope, about one inch thick, soaked in saltpetre was lit and hung at the break of the fo'c's'le; and another aft. These were used to light our cigarettes during the hours of darkness. All that had to be done was blow on the end of the rope and when it glowed red you lit your cigarette from it. The slow-match, as it was called, lasted for ages.

When leaving Plymouth Sound our life–lines were rigged before we headed out into the grey Atlantic. No more than a few miles out the big floating dock we had escorted out of Singapore appeared. The sea-going tugs were still towing her and she was escorted by a corvette. Singapore to Britain in nine months!

Quickly leaving it behind we turned to starboard, heading towards Lands End, and proceeded up the Irish Sea towards Liverpool. Of course, as usual, nobody knew where we were going but learned through the grapevine our destination was HMS EAGLET, the shore establishment at Liverpool. This was to be our home base for the next eighteen months. I bet the dockyard workers took a double- take when they beheld a mauve destroyer bearing down on them instead of a pusser's grey one!

June 1993
HMS Westcott Veterans at North Russian Convoys Reunion at Bob Smale's Hotel, Jersey. *Left to Right:*
Bob Smale : Stormy Fairweather : Bill Merry
Ginger Sawyers : Nobby Clark : Ernest Quarrie
S Farquharson Roberts

CHAPTER SEVEN.

Western Approaches

On shore leave during our short stay in Liverpool awaiting a convoy, some of us took the opportunity to get to know more of this great and historical port. Starting at Gladstone Dock, in Bootle, we took the overhead railway to the Pier Head passing numerous other docks on the way. It was great to see all the warehouses and lock-gates at each dock. There were so many ships being loaded, unloaded and repaired.

You could imagine, in days gone by, the great P & O liners leaving the dock side to the cheering of the crowds, with the bands playing as people boarded for their long journeys. Some were probably leaving forever in the hope of a better life elsewhere. Previous to that would be the great wooden ships filled with Negroes, huddled in the holds, bound for the New World as slave labour.

From the Pier Head, looking out over the River Mersey, could be seen the ferries plying to and from Birkenhead, Wallasey and New Brighton. In the river were ships at anchor awaiting a convoy. Turning towards the city centre, on the right was the Royal Liver building with the golden Liver birds on top. Next to it were the offices of the Cunard Shipping Line. Walking into the city centre past the Mersey Tunnel entrance, were St George's buildings and Lime Street station. We had a good look round the city centre and a browse round the shops before making our way back on board after a cup of tea at the Navy House.

On our return to WESTCOTT it was found that a large consignment of woollen clothing had been delivered to the ship consisting of gloves, socks, scarves and balaclavas to be shared around equally among the upper deck watchkeeping personnel. All had been knitted by the good ladies of Morecambe - a very kind gesture and I remember hoping they'd been told how much their efforts had been appreciated. Our good overcoats, issued when we first joined, had mostly long gone and the few still around were used between us to keep our legs warm while huddled up on the quarter deck. They were usually passed from watch to watch. In place of our great coats we had duffel coats with hoods, fastened by toggles. Our walking-out coat was a Burberry (a light raincoat) which was a lot more convenient and presentable.

WESTCOTT was three days in Liverpool before receiving our sailing instructions. As we ploughed our way up the Irish Sea collecting further ships from Scotland and Ireland for our convoy and, together with the rest of the escort, we continued into the Atlantic towards America and Canada. The convoy slowly zigzagged across the Atlantic. The escort did a further zigzag within the main one so the distance covered by the escort was considerable. Convoying in this manner a wide sweep with the Asdics was obtained, but due to the limited amount of fuel we could carry the distance travelled was limited. Therefore, when a little less than half our fuel had been used, we had to turn back, leaving the merchant ships at the mercy of the German U-boats, although escorts that had a longer range than us carried on whereby with the help of Sunderland flying boats the risk was reduced. However, the danger was still considerable. Usually, if we escorted a convoy out, we met one coming in when all the escort left the outgoing convoy to return guarding the one full of supplies. By the time we had met them they had usually lost a few ships to the U-boats. The gap of nearly eight hundred miles was perilous for the men of the Merchant Navy. I often thought they must have believed we were 'chicken', if they didn't understand our problems with regard to fuel.

On arrival back in Liverpool we were granted shore leave until such time as another convoy was ready to leave.

Whenever we went ashore it was obligatory to carry our gas masks with us. We also had to use the air-raid shelters when the sirens sounded. This was to set a good example to the local populace, not that they needed much encouragement. However, during one of these air raids, I was in a shelter in Bootle, skylarking with some of the girls, when the all-clear sounded and I walked out forgetting my gas mask. The next time in harbour I had strict instructions from the cox'n to go ashore and find it on pain of a slow lingering death at his bare hands if I failed to do so.

After enquiring at the shelter, I was directed to the Air Raid Wardens' office in Knowlsey Road. Here I was informed a certain Norman Nicholson had it and he lived at 23 Smollett Street. After thanking Mr Nicholson I headed for the local church of St Leonards to give thanks for saving my life and for a cup of tea and a game of billiards. Whilst engaged in my game in walked Mr Nicholson and inviting me to return with him to his home to meet his wife. They must have thought I looked hungry I was asked to stop and take high tea with them. From that point on we struck up a friendship which was to last for forty-two years until they died, Norman at the grand old age of eighty-seven and Edith, a few years later, at the age of ninety-two.

During our next trip out to meet a convoy I was working in the boiler room. With the ship rolling and tossing it was quite a job and as usual I finished up with a burnt arm. It is essential, however, to keep vital places like these properly lit. If a sight-glass broke, steam and water affected the light behind it and I would have to dry it out or replace it. All in all I got on well with the boiler-room and engine-room personnel and the more inaccessible work I would try to do in harbour. The ship was old and all the wiring could have done with replacing. It never was while I was aboard, so it was a constant battle to keep it going.

While escorting HG48 a huge explosion occurred on our starboard beam. An oil tanker had been torpedoed. Flames shot about hundred and fifty feet into the sky, after which a pall of black smoke, twice as high as the flames, covered the sky. Two minutes later all that was left was smoke.

A corvette on the starboard side, close to the scene of the event, raced to the rescue, finding two survivors. How they managed to escape was a miracle. They must have been blown straight from the bridge into the sea. I bet in a couple of weeks they would be back at sea again, poor devils. A search was made for the U-boat, but it was not located. The convoy continued on its way, each ship and individual hoping and praying it would not be their turn next.

Back in Liverpool we found the Luffwaffe had been busy bombing the area. The Liverpudlians had suffered while we had been away. I went off to see if my new found friends were all right and was pleased to find them fit and well. They gave me all the news of what had gone on in different parts of the city. I felt sorry for them, but, as with the Londoners the spirit of the Liverpudlians had not been broken and we enjoyed a cheerful chat before I had to return to my ship.

We were off again on another convoy, this time SC18. While proceeding to meet this convoy we sighted a lifeboat full of merchant seaman whose ship had been sunk a fortnight earlier. We hauled the poor beggars on board and sank their boat. It was no use any other ship finding an empty boat as it might cost the ship dearly while stopping to investigate.

The men were taken for'ard and distributed among the messes. To the five in our mess we gave our hammocks and provided electric fires to keep them warm. They were all frozen and had frost-bite. The sick bay attendant said two of them would probably lose their toes. These two sat huddled around the fire wrapped in blankets until we got them back to harbour. The only food they had was ship's biscuits. As a matter of fact, that's all we had, for we had been at sea for nearly ten days and had long since run out of fresh bread and meat. At least we had ship's cocoa and our biscuits tasted different so, along with tinned stuff, we managed fine until back in Greenock, where the survivors disembarked and went to hospital.

Before proceeding further with this story I must comment on the merchant seamen. You hear and read of the famous 'Few', who, I have no doubt, deserve every praise showered upon them, but nothing compares with the ordeals of the merchant seamen. If their ship's engines failed, which they often did, they were left on the high seas to their own devices and many became the victims of U-boats. A few ships flew barrage balloons, to protect them from the Luffwaffe, others had the odd, old gun to guard against these aircraft and surface U-boats. All were at the mercy of the elements as well as aircraft and submarines. A few got medals and a pat on the back. A lot got a cold, wet, grave. The majority just got another ship. They certainly kept us supplied all through the war. Without them we would have been in dire straits and I do believe they deserve far better recognition than has been given.

Having applied for promotion to the higher grade of leading seaman, out came my seamanship manual and I commenced studying again in preparation for my next examinations.

It was about this time, that the canteen manager absconded with all the funds. A search was made but he was never found as far as I know. For the next few days our coxswain took over until a replacement was found. The coxswain must have been worth his weight in gold, for on WESTCOTT he seemed to take on every job imaginable when the need arose.

Our next job was a bit of a fiasco. We were escorting about thirty ships back from the U.S.A. when, just as dusk was falling, we were enshrouded in thick fog and not another ship was seen through the night. Come morning the convoy had disappeared and could not be found. The skipper went mad with the officer of the watch. With W.T. silence and no other means of contact, like radar, we could not find a single ship.

After searching around for what seemed ages we were running short of fuel, so had to give up and return to port.

On arriving in Liverpool, we not only found our ships, but learned to my surprise, I had been upgraded to leading seaman. That night I wrote home telling them the good news and stitched the distinguishing badges on my different clothes. I was now in charge of the mess and of the watch on the quarter deck.

It was round about this time the Lieutenant Commander Seagrave left the ship, and Commander Bockett-Pugh took over. Things certainly changed for the new captain was a strict disciplinarian.

Later that night there was an air raid, so off I went to my post on the quarter deck as leading seaman in charge of the after-repair party. The ship, when in harbour, helped in the best way it could with the A.A. defence of Gladstone dock. Not that we were much good, because our guns would not elevate high enough. Nevertheless, we had our pom-pom gun.

The next evening I went ashore to see the Nicholsons. I was now the envy of the ship as I had an 'up-homers' base. I could stop out all night sleeping at my friends' home, if I so wished. The other poor lads had to go all the way into Liverpool to the Navy House. As for me, I went to the pictures, dances, and had the occasional night at the local.

When I arrived at the Nicholsons the whole street was closed off. I could see the bottom of the street had been shattered by a bomb and there was an unexploded bomb in the next street.

All the residents had been evacuated, where to I did not know, so off I went to the Air Raid Wardens' office to enquire. They proved to be O.K. and were staying at relatives not far away. I soon located them and a day or two later the Army defused the bomb and everybody returned to their homes.

During the week I introduced two of my shipmates, Ed Cloutman and Sid Edwards, to the Nicholsons. We all went out for the evening, during which time the two lads informed us they were going to bring their wives to live in Bootle, so that they could see them when WESTCOTT was in harbour. A few days later they arrived and introductions followed all round.

If I remember rightly, while escorting convoy SC2 the weather was atrocious. It was very cold - sou'westers, seaboots and oilskins were the rig of the day. Even then we were usually soaked to the skin. When walking to and from the quarter-deck we had to hang on to the life-lines like grim death. Many times I'd be lifted off my feet and swung into the air until the ship returned to an even keel. It was certainly a hair-raising experience.

Tragedy struck twice on the return journey. A ship was sunk in the middle of the convoy. After one of the escorts had picked up the survivors a search was made for the U-boat , but it couldn't be located. Shortly afterwards a further ship was sunk. This was also in the middle of the convoy. It was now obvious where the submarine was so the Commodore ordered the convoy to scatter, but the elusive submarine managed to escape. Later we managed to meet up with a number of ships and started to gather them together again. The faster ones had gone on ahead so when all the remainder were collected we continued on our slow way back to the UK without further mishaps.

Passing the Bar Light at the entrance to Liverpool, the skipper received a signal from shore. He then sent for the two lads, Cloutman and Edwards, who had just brought their wives up from London, together with signalman McKivett, revealing to them the contents of the signal. It appears we had only been left for a couple of days when there was an air-raid and a bomb had dropped on the house they had rented. Mrs Primrose Cloutman, her two year old daughter Margaret and Mrs Dorothy Evelyn Edwards had been killed. Mrs Doris McKivett had been injured and was in hospital. It was ironic - two of them had come from London hoping to escape the bombing there and to be near their partners. We were all shocked and heartbroken for our shipmates and found it impossible to find the right words to say as much to them in their grief. I went ashore with them, taking them to the Nicholsons. They told Sid and Eddie what had happened and that they had gone to the funeral, later taking them to see the graves.

To add further to these unfortunate times, going ashore a day or two later and passing a destroyer I watched them taking a dead sailor out of the dock. He must have been in the water some considerable time as his suit was skin tight even to his bell bottom trousers. The poor devil must have been blown into the dock during an air raid.

It was now Christmas. Port watch was given leave and when they returned it was the turn of the starboard watch to have the New Year. While starboard watch was on leave it gave us the opportunity to have a good clean up and paint the mess deck. I slapped gallons of red lead under the lockers, hoping the cockroaches would stick to the paint, but they never did and seemed to thrive on red lead. As well as painting the mess deck it was a good time to do some dhobying and get down to a bit of make and mend. This was always a chore to most of us.

Air-raids were still in progress in Liverpool. I remember one night assisting the children and old people into air raid shelters that had been built in the streets. There were bunks for children to sleep in whilst the older people sat on forms. Many of the older people would not go in the shelters. They preferred to say at home, sitting under the stairs.

This was the situation this particular night. After seeing all the people I could into the shelter, I went to my friends' house. Mr and Mrs Nicholson were on duty as wardens, but, under the stairs, were Grandma and the two children, so I stayed with them, chatting and playing games. Then a bomb dropped in the next street. The explosion caused the window frames to be blown in, so there I was, trying to repair the damage, pushing window frames back and, at the same time, praying there would be no more bombs.

Earlier that year the two Nicholson children, like thousands more, had been evacuated to places of safety away from the city. The boy, Eric, went to Southport and the girl, Norma, to a farm in North Wales. Mother missed the children and the children were very homesick so they were soon back together again, having decided it was better to chance it. At least the family were together. If anything happened to one it would happen to them all.

The ship's catering was easier now. With the rationing and shortage of food, the selection for meals was limited, but the mess was at least getting a good return on the allowance. I used to watch the chef in the officers' galley make some very appetising meals out of nothing and wished I could do the same. When all was quiet at night we would scrounge round the officers' galley to see what they had going for their meals, but everything was taken away or locked up.

Mind you, that was the only job the chef had to do all day, other than passing up shells and cordite during the time we were firing our guns, which was not that often. However, I tried my best at catering with what was available.

I did read a book written by an officer in which he said "The meals on board the V & W class destroyers were marvellous." I can only say that if he had been in our mess for a month or two he'd have written a very different book.

On our next outward bound convoy we had to escort about thirty-five ships. This was in January and the reference number for the convoy was OE 51. WESTCOTT was in company with HMS BLUEBELL, HMS CANDYTUFT, HMS SCIMITAR and HMS SKATE. During the second dog watch I was in the stokers' mess deck when there was an almighty crash. Someone shouted. "We've been hit," and there was a mad race to the ladder. Some tried to get through a hatch, two at a time, trapping themselves in the process. After sorting themselves out I was able to get out of the mess deck and found that the corvette, HMS BLUEBELL. had collided with our starboard side and impaled herself in our boiler-room.

Apparently, BLUEBELL and WESTCOTT got a contact on a submarine and were both going into the attack at the same time, when they collided as described. When BLUEBELL drew back, water flooded into our No1 boiler room. Stokers wasted no time in shoring up the bulkheads while the remainder of the crew stood at "Abandon Ship" stations. After the stokers had finished we stood down and the ship then proceeded slowly back to Londonderry, along with BLUEBELL, for repairs.

This was the last we saw of BLUEBELL and when we next heard about her was in February 1944. BLUEBELL had been hit by a torpedo from U-711 while on a Russian convoy and, out of a crew of ninety, only one survived.

On arrival in Londonderry the fire tenders were waiting and as soon as we docked firemen began to pump the water out, using timbers down the side to prevent the sea getting in again. The crumpled plates were then cut away and further timbers fitted on the inside, and, finally, the gap between the two sets of timbers was blocked with concrete.

While this temporary work was being carried out we went ashore to look around Londonderry. The first thing that struck me were the houses. They all seemed to have crosses above their doors. Of course they must have been strong Catholics. In the public houses no women were to be seen, or so it seemed, until one night, on leaving, I looked into a small room, and there they all were, drinking in secret.

In the main street was a rifle gallery. As it happened, they were having a competition so I joined in and did rather well.

By the end of the second week I had reached the final, in which, sad to say, I was beaten by two points. By this time all the mess knew about it and came to watch and to help me spend my winnings, which was one pound. At least we had a good night out dancing and fraternising with the local colleens.

I remember going to the pictures with one of my mates. He was almost bald and to my way of thinking didn't have much going for him. He boasted he could get any women he wanted, so I bet he couldn't. When we got into the pictures we sat behind some girls. He leaned forward and started to tickle the girl in front of him behind the ears and the nape of the neck. As soon as the pictures were over he was walking her home. I was amazed and also lost my bet, but don't think I've ever been able to master that technique myself.

While in Londonderry, Lord Louis Mountbatton came on a flying visit and, of course, all ships in harbour had to provide a contingent of men for parading. A great ceremony and march-past was held. Fortunately, I found myself something important to do in the engine room and missed it all.

Once the temporary repairs had been completed WESTCOTT set sail for Liverpool, where, to my dismay and the delight of the rest of the crew, we went into Herculean dock. It was much nearer the city centre and much further away from Bootle. However, I made out all right. Norman Nicholson worked in the dockyard and quickly found me, whereby there was great rejoicing in Smollett Street that day.

The ship went into dry dock and the concrete knocked away. New plates were riveted in place, the boiler was cleaned, and other jobs done. As it was estimated this would take about five weeks, each watch was given ten days leave.

Air raids on Liverpool had now virtually stopped. Rationing was the problem foremost in peoples' minds. Coupons and dockets were required for nearly everything and it all had to be queued for. Cigarettes were very difficult to get and if you weren't the shopkeeper's flavour of the day, you had to queue for hours. On board ship as far as cigarettes were concerned we were not too badly off, because duty free was a big advantage. My monthly allowance of tinned tobacco ('ticklers') was turned over to Norman Nicholson to help him out and he got quite expert at rolling his own cigarettes.

After both watches had had their leave it was seen that the work would still take a while to complete, so each watch was given a further week's leave. What the folks at home thought I do not know, but I was running short of money so was glad to be back on board ship. Most of my school mates were now away in the forces so things were very different - being by yourself could be boring so I was glad to get back to WESTCOTT after seven days.

But as the ship was still not ready the rest of my shore leave was spent in Bootle. I remember on Saturday I went to the Pier Head to meet Norman Nicholson and his brother-in-law Jack Newall. Jack was a tug master and seemed to be a law unto himself. He was in possession of a deep sea masters certificate and showed me around his tug in the Royal Albert dock. It was most interesting to see how those men lived aboard such a small, but sturdy craft.

On completion of repairs HMS WESTCOTT was assigned to the 7th Escort Group, and on return to Gladstone dock, we were invaded by a film crew. The object was to take films of the depth charges as they exploded in fifty feet of water. Of course, we couldn't waste depth charges just for the sake of some pictures so they had to wait for the real thing. They were kept on tenter-hooks most of the time. Each time we got an echo, up they would come, set up the tripod and camera, only to be disappointed when it turned out to be a false alarm. Towards the end of the journey they were rewarded. We got a firm contact. HMS WISHART was in on the engagement so it was ideal for the film crew. In came the imposing WISHART. She swerved and fired a pattern of five depth charges. It was then our turn, so the film crew dashed to the stern with their equipment and got all the pictures they wanted. I thought I might be a film star, dashing around, setting the charges, but all they were after was the big splash. I am afraid a picture of picking up U-boat survivors never materialised as the U-boat escaped. When we returned to harbour they filmed the pom-pom gun crew with their anti-flash gear on, taking a picture of them from the dock side. I was given to understand it was for the film 'In Which We Serve' or, maybe 'The Cruel Sea'. Never did learn more than than.

It was May 23rd 1941 and we were off to Iceland in order to fetch home a large convoy containing troopships. Before leaving, a distinguished writer of that time, boarded WESTCOTT as war correspondent to a national newspaper. He was billeted in the captain's day cabin. While on watch I could see him through the ward-room hatch. He never seemed to be without a glass of gin in his hand. Perhaps he was nervous.

Picking up the convoy just off Iceland we proceeded to escort it back to the U.K. A signal was received that the German battleship BISMARCK and the heavy cruiser PRINZ EUGEN had left their lair in Norway and were heading into the North Atlantic. It was assumed that the objective of these two mighty ships was the convoy we were escorting. They certainly had come out as surface raiders to play havoc with our shipping.

WESTCOTT had closed up at action stations and doubled the lookouts. A man was sent up into the crow's nest and everyone was warned to be ready at a moment's notice. A buzz then went round the ship that the battle cruiser HMS HOOD and the new battleship HMS PRINCE OF WALES were sailing to engage the enemy, but it was still essential that we stay in this sort of readiness as long as it was considered necessary.

The following day, May 24th 1941, we were devastated to learn that the might HOOD had been sunk and PRINCE OF WALES damaged. It was not long before we learned that all 1,400 men aboard HOOD, except for three, had been lost in this mind-boggling disaster. All aboard WESTCOTT were stunned. This catastrophe was beyond our comprehension and HOOD was the apple of every sailor's eye. It could be our turn next, for everyone was convinced it was our convoy the Germans were after.

The Commodore immediately ordered the convoy to scatter. The fastest merchant ships went quickly on their way and the slower ones were accompanied by the corvettes as best they could.

We were then told over the loud hailer that BISMARCK and PRINZ EUGEN were only one hundred miles away and we were travelling at full speed ahead to engage them. His remarks on the bridge, as we learned later from the signalman, were “If only I can get a torpedo attack in”. The crew were called to action stations. Up went the battle flag. Repair parties went to their stations. The canteen manager, stokers that were not on watch below, signalmen, telegraphists and stewards were all engaged in battening-down, and opening up the shell rooms and magazines. Pistols were fitted in the torpedoes and they were trained outboard ready for use. Shells and cordite began to arrive at the guns. The stokers below were working their hardest to keep any trace of smoke from becoming visible to the enemy and every one that was available became a lookout. It was estimated that, at our speed, we should see BISMARCK within four hours, or less.

It was now time to reflect on what could happen and our hearts went into out boots. The thought of engaging BISMARCK alone was a self-destructive venture, but PRINZ EUGEN as well, left little speculation on its outcome. If the enemy was closing in on us at the same speed the time to meet them would be much shorter than four hours. I expect a few prayers were said as we sped towards the enemy ships. Those preparing for the engagement did not have much time to think, but we that were repair parties, etc. let our thoughts and imaginations run away. I always felt sorry for those shut away in those small shell and cordite rooms. At least we on the upper deck could see what was going on and the feeling of being trapped was eliminated. Onward we continued, watching the wake of the ship as we surged forward. But - after four hours - nothing! What had happened? To the disappointment of the captain, and to our relief, we received a signal that BISMARCK and PRINZ EUGEN were steaming away and not towards us. They must be at least one hundred miles away from us still. Because of our fuel situation we were ordered back to round up the convoy and resume our duties. As we stood down from action stations and the shells and cordite were being returned to their respective storage places, little sighs of relief and a little cheer or two could be heard. So ended one more moment in the glorious history of HMS WESTCOTT. After all, it isn't every day that a brand new, mighty battleship and heavy cruiser turns tail and runs from an itty-bitty, over-aged destroyer!

The final chapter in the story of BISMARCK and PRINZ EUGEN is well known. After the sinking of HMS HOOD every available ship in the British Navy was sent to look for those two German ships. They had to be sunk to regain the honour of the Navy. Both were finally spotted by aircraft and, after a chase of 1,750 miles, were caught by HMS KING GEORGE V, HMS RODNEY and HMS DORSETSHIRE along with escorting destroyers. A torpedo attack was launched. A torpedo hit the stern of BISMARCK and she lost way. RODNEY and KING GEORGE V silenced her gun fire and torpedoes from HMS DORSETSHIRE finally sank her. During this melee PRINZ EUGEN escaped to the French port of Brest.

The result of the engagement stopped the surface raiders and saved a lot of merchant ships from being sunk.

All this time, the war correspondent had stood in amazement trying to take it all in. He had not realised that the cordite and shell rooms were under his feet. What a story he would have to tell his readers - and he did! Later I read in the newspaper of his great escape. My, that man deserved a medal. I bet he downed a few more gins after he had got over the shock. When we arrived back in Liverpool the news of the sinking of the battle cruiser HOOD was in the papers. This was a most depressing set-back in the war for the British people, and we of the British Navy in particular.

On July 18th 1941 WESTCOTT formed part of the escort to convoy OB364. This consisted of about thirty ships. The convoy had barrage balloons to protect it from aircraft, when on the horizon appeared two Focke Wulf Condors. They seemed to hover there, probably sending messages to the submarine wolf packs. There was nothing much we could do except watch, as they were too far away. At least we were forewarned so were forearmed and closed up at action stations.

Maybe because U-boats were not in the vicinity, one of these large aircraft decided to attack. Down the centre of the convoy it came, its engines roaring. Every ship opened up with their guns. Still it came ominously on, then it dropped its bombs hitting the SS PILAR DE LARRINAGA on the bridge. Then, as it turned away to starboard, one of the merchant ships hit it with gunfire and the tip of its wing touched the barrage balloon wire. Down it crashed. As it hit the water it turned into a massive bomb blowing itself to smithereens. A great cheer went up. Being the nearest to the stricken ship we raced to the scene and passed what was left of the Focke Wulf. All I saw was the leg of a German inside a jack boot.

Approaching the PILAR DE LARRINAGA we could see a fire raging underneath the bridge. Her water main had been fractured and the crew helpless to engage the fire, so we went alongside using our own hoses to tackle it. Then, a portable pump was put on board along with half a dozen matelots to assist the crew.

Everyone on the bridge of the PILAR DE LARRINAGA had been killed. These were all the officers and the lookouts. The only officer left was the engineering officer, who was, of course, below in the engine room. The lads who had been put on board got to the base of the fire under the bridge and started to tackle it with the bridge just like a frying pan.

When the crew of the merchant ship and our lads had the fire under control and the deck had cooled, a clearing-up operation was put in hand. The dead were lowed to the deck below and their shipmates respectfully committed their bodies to the deep after they had got under way. The injured were transferred to WESTCOTT.

On board the merchant ship there was nobody left to navigate, so, after all our men were back aboard, the skipper put an officer and signalman McKivett aboard. WESTCOTT proceeded to escort SS PILAR DE LARRINAGA back to England. Because all the steering gear on the bridge had been blown away, commands had to be relayed by word of mouth to the engine room. Doing this for two or three hundred miles was a feat on its own, and if anybody deserved a medal it was those two, but, like many more, they were forgotten.

After seeing the merchant ship safely into harbour we went to Liverpool to have slight hull damage repaired, after which we were transferred to Albert Dock. Here dockyard workers streamed on board, removed 'A gun' from the fo'c's'le and replaced it with a Spigot Gun, later called a Hedgehog Gun. It consisted of twenty four bombs mounted on a rectangular cradle for'ard of the bridge. It fired ahead in an oval pattern. Each of the bombs had a thirty seven pound charge of high explosive with a contact fuse. The range was one cable and was effective down to 1200 feet.

When the job was completed an admiral, with his aide and a few boffins, came on board and we set sail for Greenock. There a submarine awaited us fitted with a ninety-foot mast.

Together, we sailed into the Irish sea to test this new weapon. First, a dummy pattern of bombs were fired ahead of the ship for the back-room boy, the admiral and the submarine captain to see. The submarine then dived until only a small portion of the mast was visible at which we fired more dummy bombs. The submarine captain signalled he had been hit by releasing a smoke canister. Later the submarine crew told us they heard the bombs hit and realised this was a new anti submarine weapon.

When we returned to harbour it was decided to give the crew practice at loading the Hedgehog gun. AB Blower was chosen and while sliding the bomb on to the spigot it fired. The dummy bomb shot into the air taking half Able Seaman Blower's hand with it and ending his career in about a second. He was rushed to hospital and that was the last we saw of him.

I believe he was seen some time later working in his father's greengrocer's shop and coping reasonably well.

An investigation took place as to what had happened. Some thought it was left switched on, others that it had residual magnetism, and finally that a hair wire in the gun had detached itself and that the ship's vibrations had triggered it off. No doubt the back-room boys would sort it out, but that was not much good to the poor victim.

After this episode we returned to Liverpool. On arrival at the Pier Head, live bombs were fitted and we went straight out again near to the Bar Light, where there was a sunken wreck and fired the bombs. We obviously hit it because hundreds of stunned fish came to the surface. The skipper gave permission to lower the whalers and harvest the fish. A good fresh fish was most welcome and went down well for supper that evening. The whalers' crew collected enough to say that if only we could have kept them fresh there would have been enough to see us through to the end of the war!

Arriving back in Liverpool the boffins left us, but not before enjoying a goodly portion of our fish and chips. We had so much fish it was decided to distribute them among some of the other ships nearby. I decided to take a bucketful to my friends in Bootle. Boarding the Overhead Railway to Seaforth I carted that heavy bucket of fish to Smollett Street, to find Granny was the only person at home for the others had gone to the pictures. After putting the fish into the sink, I suggested that Mrs Nicholson should share them with her friends in the street, and returned to WESTCOTT with my empty bucket.

The Spigot gun was then removed, the ship returned to normal, with our own 4" gun back in its rightful place. It was a pity they did not put an anti-aircraft gun there instead. It was badly needed.

During this spell in Liverpool I got toothache and was sent to HMS EAGLET the H.Q. shore establishment where they had a dentist in residence. He must have had dirty instruments, as the next day I was in a worse state than before being sent to him for treatment. The following day I was rolling on the deck in agony with a badly swollen face and was sent back to the dentist by our sick bay tiffy. My gum was lanced and I was kept in EAGLET's sick bay overnight.

Come morning it was found that WESTCOTT had left and I was to be sent to meet her via the R.T.O on Lime Street station. The Army then sent me on by troop train to Glasgow.

I got on well with the soldiers in our carriage. They wanted to know where I had been and what I had done. (Well, that took up most of the five hour journey!) They said they would not be in the Navy for all the tea in China, on the basis that if you went into action you had two ways of dying, either being killed on the ship or drowning in the sea. They had only one, but even so I think any matelot preferred the 'Andrew' to the 'Kate'!

On arriving in Glasgow I was transferred to a lorry going to Gourock, where I joined my ship. That night about seven of us went to the Palais de Dance. It was a big place and had a good band. A good time was had by all and we returned to the ship by taxi. How all seven of us managed to get into that taxi, I will never know.

In October WESTCOTT was temporary acting senior officer's ship of the First Escort Group, escorting convoy ON.28. This convoy was relatively quiet and no ships were lost. In December we did a further two convoys WS 14 and HG 76. The seas were terrible. Steaming south-west to meet the convoy the ship seemed to lift out of the water on the crest of one wave, crashing down onto the next, on and on, for what seemed an eternity. The ship shuddered so much it was a wonder there was any ship left. On reaching the convoy we turned to face worse conditions. Zig-zagging our way back, we would get broad side on to the storm, rolling so much it was feared the old girl might turn over. To the merchant ships we must have looked like a there-you-see it, there-you-don't mirage bobbing about on the ocean, for most of their ships were so much bigger than WESTCOTT. At least, when these conditions prevailed it was impossible for the U-boats to get an attack together. From their point of view when a ship came into periscope vision it was immediately blocked out by the high waves. They were unable to sight on their target long enough to hope to fire a torpedo accurately. There would probably be other variables that I wasn't aware of. Therefore, bad weather was good for protecting merchant ships.

If the weather was reasonable on a quiet trip some of the crew would play cards, dominoes, chess or draughts. Others would play maj jong or uckers, a sophisticated game of ludo. A great many would be writing home or doing their dhobying or just sitting down spinning yarns. I liked to play draughts and bezique. In the evening a game of tombola was usually organised. In harbour, as well as playing all these games, we played football.

One of the lads was mad on classical music. Knowing I liked it too he brought some records back from home and when all had gone ashore on a Saturday we used to sit on the wash down lockers at the break of the fo'c's'le listening to Gigli and Caruso. I brought from home Dance of the Hours, Largo and a few more, which we played on our old mess wind-up gramophone. Those were the days!

Returning with convoy, WS 14 we docked at Greenock again. Believing my friends in Liverpool might be wondering if anything had happened to me, I wrote them a letter to let them know I was still in the land of the living.

Although we did not know it at the time, convoy HG 76 was to be our last for a while for we were to be transferred to H force in the Mediterranean. It was December and the weather was very cold. Sailing towards Iceland to meet our convoy we sat in our little cluster on the quarter deck shivering with cold. Times like those you don't wish to remember. Icicles were hanging everywhere. Approaching Iceland I saw my first iceberg, just off Reykjavik. It was a magnificent sight, glittering white with sheer sides. It made us feel so insignificant. Considering only one third of it could be seen, with the other two thirds under the water, its size must have been immense. We sailed around it to discover if any U-boats were lurking at the other side, using it as cover while awaiting the convoy. One of the seamen was in the crow's nest. His view of this awesome sight must have been marvellous. The seamen did a spell of one or two hours each in the crow's nest where it must have been twice as bitter than on deck. Many things seen during our time convoying gave us the 'collywobbles' as we watched schools of whales and porpoises following us for miles. Away in the distance a whale could look awfully like a submarine, and the fluorescent wake of a porpoise could certainly look like a torpedo. Another thing was the disposal of waste. This had to be done at night because sea gulls would trail your ship all day awaiting scraps and a flock of sea gulls could well disclose our whereabouts to any U-boat in the vicinity.

Eventually the convoy appeared. Once again we zigzagged our way back. The conditions of this convoy were the same as the previous ones, only this time two stragglers had to be left behind with only one escort to protect them. We could not afford to jeopardise the remainder of the convoy waiting for them to do repairs. We just had to hope they would arrive home safely. On reaching Liverpool a message was received that we should proceed to Devonport after re-fuelling.

CHAPTER EIGHT
Promotion

On arrival in Devonport we went into dry dock where the ship's bottom was inspected and the keel found to be bent and wrinkled - thanks to the constant punishment meted out over the years by the stormy waters of the world. The dockyard decided nothing could be done about it, so after everything below the waterline had been scraped and painted with a couple of coats of anti-foul compound, she carried on with her 'crinkly' keel until her RN days were over. In the meantime and while in dry-dock an up-dated Asdic dome was fitted to that 'corrugated' keel, Y gun was removed and replaced by a Bofor gun. Oerlikon guns were fitted either side of the bridge and machine gun supports welded to the deck, amidships. Along with the pom-pom guns our anti-aircraft defences were much improved.

A degaussing cable was fitted around the ship as a protection against magnetic mines. This was a more permanent job. A small current was passed through the cable to keep the ship magnetically neutralised. The ship was fitted with emergency lighting everywhere consisting of low voltage lights, like miners' lanterns, hung from the deck head. An electric supply was connected to them. If the mains supply was interrupted, the lights came on automatically. These were a great help to those that worked in the boiler rooms, shell rooms and other places that relied completely on artificial lighting. It meant more work for those who had to maintain battery back-up for the emergency lighting. Not to be outdone, the stokers were doing yet another boiler clean.

Starboard watch went on leave. During this time I was sent on board the aircraft carrier HMS INDOMITABLE to qualify for leading seaman, and taken from one cabin to another to be examined on boat work, anchor work, signals, Morse code, seamanship and the rest of the requirements.

Came my turn to go on leave I went as a full-blown leading seaman (a killick) and thought I would spend a few days with my family in Darlington and the rest with my friends in Liverpool. However, that never transpired for after a couple of days came a recall telegram, that meant returning to my ship straight away. Climbing aboard I noticed a few new faces.

The ship already had steam up, and the gyroscope was running. The shore supply was then disconnected and the ships own system energised.. WESTCOTT quietly left harbour at Devonport and was soon passing Plymouth Hoe. Once out at sea the skipper decided to try out our new armament. The Oerlikons and Bofor guns were very good. The tracer bullets from the Oerlikon guns would be a great help to whoever was firing them. In order to maintain fire-power in an emergency, the torpedoemen stationed on the quarter deck were given instruction and shown how to use them.

During our activities on the upper deck the stokers were busy below. There was never a dull moment for them. After the boiler clean in which all the tubes were cleaned out, a laborious task in itself, the front of the boilers then received their attention. Black lead was applied, just like mother used to do to the fire place, only on a vastly larger scale.

After this job had been completed all brass work was polished until you could see your face in it, and there was quite a lot of it to do. When that was done the stokers burnished the deck on which they stood with wire brushes. The place was so clean when they had finished you could eat a meal off the deck.

While crossing the Bay of Biscay our new Asdics made contact on a U-boat. We went into the attack, but the U-boat evaded us. We turned and attacked again. Then the U-boat seemed to disappear. We stopped engines, going into a listening watch. While in this situation everyone had to be as quiet as possible, especially the engine room staff - no dropping of spanners, etc. In order to keep the ship in a state of readiness the dynamos had to be kept running, but it was amazing how quiet it could get.

Of course, the U-boat was doing the same thing. They, however, could do it much better, having batteries to keep their instruments and lighting on. As soon as we heard a sound we went into action again. The U-boat knew the enemy was still above them, daring them to make a move. This cat and mouse game lasted for forty-eight hours until our fuel was running low and we had to leave.

The U-boat's crew must have been relieved when they heard us receding from them, but not for long, as we had sent a coded signal to Gibraltar and a Catalina aircraft had been sent out. When the U-boat surfaced for air, it was sunk. Maybe it would have been better for them to have surrendered to us. At least we could have picked up their survivors. As it was they probably all drowned.

From the time we left Devonport until we reached Gibraltar one of the new intake was desperately seasick. He lay on a sack of potatoes at the break of the fo'c's'le not daring to go to the mess. At least he was getting fresh air and was near the heads. Every so often he ran to the ship's side to be sick. As a fighting member of the ship's company the poor lad was absolutely useless. He could not do a thing at sea, he was so ill.

In harbour when it was piped 'ship under four hours sailing', he would turn green. After a month of this the doctor decided to send him back to Britain, where, I am sure, he would have been more useful to the war effort.

It was Christmas day when we reached Gibraltar. I think it was the worst Christmas we ever had. Dinner was corned beef, mashed potatoes and peas. The lads were cheesed off with the apparent lack of interest in our well-being. It never seemed to improve. When the skipper did his rounds to wish us all a Happy Christmas he was left in no doubt about our feelings. This seemed to be the turning point and things started to improve after that.

During our stay in Gibraltar we re-fuelled the ship, and had our depth charges replaced. We then set sail with other destroyers into the Mediterranean, escorting the aircraft carrier, HMS VICTORIOUS. She was a magnificent ship. On her flight deck were about forty aircraft. Half way to Malta these aircraft took off heading for the defence of Malta or the Middle East. The Maltese certainly needed them at the time.

Once the aircraft had gone we turned around to go back to Gibraltar. Conditions in the Med. were a lot calmer than in the Atlantic. I bet the crew of VICTORIOUS could hardly feel a ripple on that great ship.

During this trip one of the lads on my watch asked me to help him with studying for his seamanship examinations as he wished to become an officer. He had all the academic qualifications, so, armed with the seamanship manual, I introduced a question and answer session every time we were on watch together.

On reaching Gibraltar we could see a huge fire in the dockyard area and on getting closer we found it was a motor torpedo boat parked ashore on chocks. The dockyard fire brigade were in attendance, but it was a hopeless task. The Spanish dockyard workers were responsible for a great deal of the sabotage we suffered in Gibraltar. They came across from La Linea to work as there was nothing for them in Spain. They would bring incendiary devices with them and place them where they could do most damage. Yes, there were no shortage of people in those days anxious to harm our war effort.

Our next trip out was with HMS EAGLE and HMS ARGUS. While with these two ships the Luffwaffe decided to pay us a visit in the form of a single aircraft. I do not know whether he was just out on patrol when he sighted us or not, but he came in and dropped a few bombs which did no harm, and then left. I suppose he was frantically calling for assistance or reporting our position. However, our task had been completed and we turned back towards Gibraltar without any further incident.

Whilst in harbour I had an accident. When using the ladders to get from the bridge to the fo'c's'le or from the fo'c's'le to the iron deck below, I would race down them by grabbing hold of the handrails, lifting my feet off the treads and using my hands to slide down the ladder with feet in the air. I thought I was good at it until one day, I misjudged my grip and hit the bottom of my spine on every rung. Collapsing at the bottom of the ladder, I could not get up, and had to be taken to hospital by ambulance. I was X-rayed, kept in for three days, but fortunately only badly bruised. But it put paid to flying down ladders throughout the rest of my naval career.

CHAPTER NINE.

A Battle of Wits with a U-boat Pack

For our next trip out, instead of going into the Mediterranean we went into the Atlantic. Great, we thought, we are off to South Africa. It would be lovely to see either Durban or Cape Town. I had heard so many good reports of these places and was looking forward to a visit; but no such luck

Laden with one thousand troops and munitions, SS LLANGIBBY CASTLE was in convoy W.S.15, nearing the Azores when she was torpedoed in the stern by U-boat 402. Leaving the convoy she made her own way to Horta, on the Portuguese islands of the Azores, for temporary repairs. Although there was a large hole in her stern and her steering gear was wrecked she was still able to maintain steerage way and survive an attack by a German Focke Wulfe aircraft. She arrived in Horta on January 19th 1942, without further incident.

One thousand miles away leaving Gibraltar was HMS WESTCOTT, under the command of Commander L.H. Bockett-Pugh, HMS CROOME, and HMS EXMOOR; these destroyers were dispatched to escort the crippled troopship back to Gibraltar. They arrived in Horta on the afternoon of February 1st. WESTCOTT went straight into Horta harbour to re-fuel and, at the same time, re-provision. Fresh pineapples were a very welcome treat. Whilst there, Commander Bockett-Pugh went to see the Captain of the LLANGIBBY CASTLE and, with the master of the tug THAMES, they discussed tactics.

WESTCOTT, on leaving the harbour, directed CROOME and EXMOOR to go into Horta to re-fuel. When fuelling was completed, CROOME and EXMOOR joined WESTCOTT. Expecting U-boats to be lying in wait at both ends of the channel by which LLANGIBBY CASTLE would have to leave Horta, WESTCOTT stationed EXMOOR at the northern end and CROOME at the southern, WESTCOTT steered north and, after meeting EXMOOR, about midnight proceeded round the Island of Fayal to join CROOME.

At 0745hrs on February 2nd, CROOME obtained contact in a position four or five miles south-west of St Mattheus point on Pico Island WESTCOTT closed and both ships lay-to, trying to classify the echo. Eventually both ships agreed that it wasn't a sub and, with starboard wheel on, WESTCOTT left.

Almost at once WESTCOTT sighted the conning tower of a U-boat on the starboard bow. Immediately, the captain increased speed to ram. However, owing to her high speed, WESTCOTT sheared off at the last minute and fired a pattern of depth charges. Swiftly turning, she made a second run, hitting U581 a glancing blow sufficient to sink her.

The crew of the U-boat were now in the water and WESTCOTT began to pick up survivors, 39 in all. The U-boat captain's name was Werner Pfeifer and the engineering officer was Helmut Krummel. He was the only German that did the Nazi salute, on putting his foot aboard the WESTCOTT. At this, the bosun nearly broke his arm with the butt of his revolver. Reports from the crew afterwards seemed to suggest that Helmut Krummelk was a Gestapo agent.

It was discovered later from HMS CROOME, who picked up a further four survivors, that some men were in the water when the depth charges exploded. This did considerable damage to their lungs, unfortunately.

Slowly and awkwardly, LLANGIBBY CASTLE came out of harbour. Steering somewhat haphazardly she steamed east-south-east down the channel between Pico Island and San Jorge Island. Because of adverse conditions the skipper of LLANGIBBY CASTLE reluctantly accepted a tow from the sea-going tug THAMES and thus we proceeded on our way towards Gibraltar at about 8 knots.

With over a thousand lookouts aboard these ships it was thought inconceivable we would sight a U-boat, but the U-boat commanders had other ideas. They were determined not to let us pass and we were just as determined to get through.

With five or six U-boats in the vicinity, the advantage was on our side. The job looked precarious. Regardless of the great danger, this gallant little convoy continued its way into the path of these U-boats who were waiting for the kill. Up would pop a periscope ahead of us. Everyone saw it, and wondered what our skipper would do next. Precisely nothing was the answer. We kept our position, tightly protecting our ward. If we had gone into the attack, we would have had to move our position and another U-boat would surely be waiting for the kill. As we passed over the position a pattern of depth charges were fired and we continued on. Yet again, other periscopes were seen.

Along with us the Hunt Class destroyers were doing the same. Everyone gritted their teeth and kept their fingers crossed as we passed through these traumatic onslaughts. The U-boats fired torpedoes at the unfortunate ship, but, luckily, they missed.

Day by day, the escort, when within hailing distance, cheered LLANGIBBY CASTLE on. The packed troops in her battered hull assembled on deck to cheer us also. Together we slowly progressed towards Gibraltar on this daunting mission. At each dawn her master drew a deep breath of surprise to see himself still captain of his beloved ship.

Passing by and over those U-boats, our chances seemed to be getting better as we cautiously moved through those dangerous waters. We would have liked to think we got another U-boat, but could not stop to find out. After four days we approached Gibraltar at last. WESTCOTT, CROOME and EXMOOR had run out of depth charges so other destroyers in Gibraltar were sent out to assist us make the final limp home.

LLANGIBBY CASTLE seemed, said a witness, to tuck her skirts between her legs and sprint like a marathon runner to the finishing line. With the destroyer crews cheering, the Marine's band aboard HMS NELSON playing 'See The Conquering Hero Comes' and ships' whistles blowing, she careered blindly into the shelter of the Gibraltar breakwater and dropped anchor.

A ship still and all safe on board!

CHAPTER TEN.

Operating from Gibraltar.

After disembarking the German prisoners at Gibraltar it was dry dock for WESTCOTT. Everyone was looking forward to a long rest and a 'stock-survey' around the local bars, providing we could find the wherewithal!.

Unfortunately, there were a couple of fatal accidents to mar our stay in dry dock. One was a seaman returning to the ship who mistakenly took the wrong opening to where the gang-plank led to the ship and fell all the way down to the bottom of the dock. On hearing his cries a rescue was mounted. He was rushed to hospital but sadly died soon afterwards.

Then, after the repairs had been completed, WESTCOTT was getting up steam preparing for sea, when a safety valve blew off in the engine-room while a stoker P.O. was tightening it. Super-heated steam blasted into his face and he was rushed to hospital, but died soon afterwards. These two tragic accidents marred what should have been a refreshing break.

Our next venture was with the American aircraft carrier USS WASP. We all had heard how Americans boasted about having things bigger and better than anyone else. In this case it was true. WASP was huge. Ninety aircraft were lined up on her flight deck and she was truly the finest carrier I had ever seen, a ship of which the Americans were justifiably proud. If you consider HMS ARGUS carried about 10 aircraft, HMS EAGLE about 35 and HMS ILLUSTRIOUS 56, that one American ship was doing the job of three of ours. Her turn of speed was great and within a couple of days aircraft were winging their way to Malta and the Middle East. The distance of all the 'club runs', which these trips were called, into the Mediterranean, was usually limited to the limit of the German aircraft range. That is, the carriers flew off the aircraft and turned back before they came within range of most of the enemy aircraft. This had been adequate to the needs of our aircraft going to Malta, fuel wise.

My twenty-third birthday occurred on this trip, but no 'sippers' of rum this time except my own. I had now completed five years service. Back at Gibraltar we provision and re-fuelled. There was a quick turn around and out again, this time with the aircraft carrier HMS EAGLE.

The sea was much more kind to us those days. The blue Mediterranean was living up to its name. The sunsets and sunrises were a sight to behold. I would recommend a cruise on the Mediterranean to anyone (now that we've cleared it of U-boats!)

Returning to Gibraltar we found that a destroyer secured astern of the aircraft carrier HMS EAGLE had been blown up and almost sunk. It was only being held up by another ship alongside it and its own cables attached to the quay side. Apparently, our Spanish "friends" had placed a small charge inside a depth charge which blew the whole thing up. The idea was to create as much damage as possible to the aircraft carrier, but they did not succeed. I was told one of the depth charges went clean over EAGLE and into the water. Fortunately, no one was hurt as the depth charges were not primed. After this episode most of the destroyers had to anchor in the harbour or tie up to buoys to prevent the Spanish saboteurs from getting on board. But it meant that anybody going ashore would need to catch the harbour 'trot'boat.

There were several more trips into the Mediterranean with aircraft carriers. During one of these excursions long range aircraft attempted a raid on us. They were probably Focke Wulf Condors. As it happened, our fighter aircraft from EAGLE were up and soon chased them off, but had to land and refuel before proceeding to Malta. It was evening when we arrived back at Gibraltar and there was an air raid in progress. Instead of getting involved we stood off-shore watching the proceedings. It was like a fireworks display for the Royal Artillery A.A. gunners covered the sky with exploding shells and tracers. I doubted whether anything could get through. As far as we could make out nothing did, much to the disappointment of the Spanish, I am sure. After the raid we went in, finding all was well.

The escort of aircraft carriers along with anti-submarine patrols continued for the next few months, until June 1942, when Malta convoys were decided upon to relieve the beleaguered island of Malta. The situation was getting so desperate that something had to be done. Air-raids were so bad only our fastest ships, like HMS WELSHMAN, could get through.

CHAPTER ELEVEN.

Operation Harpoon.

Dawn was breaking and the silhouettes of ships were appearing, twenty in all. Six were merchant ships, the remainder were the escort. This was a convoy of ships travelling at 15 knots.

On WESTCOTT's bridge stood the skipper, the first lieutenant, a signalman, the port lookout, the starboard lookout, and me. The signalman spotted the Luftwaffe coming over the horizon. "Aircraft ahead, Sir" he reported. "More aircraft on port beam, Sir" shouted the port lookout. The first lieutenant raised his binoculars to his eyes and confirmed it was so. The skipper looked, and said, "My God, here they come." In came the aircraft, the roar of their engines growing ever louder. They were high-level bombers and torpedo-bombers. We quaked in our shoes.

The year was 1942 and the date June 13th. The raid on this convoy, which was making its way to Malta, was just the beginning. It continued all day.

The needs of Malta were great. There was hardly any food, no fuel or munitions. For months she had been at the mercy of the Luftwaffe, day and night, and the only help she was getting was from the fast mine-laying cruiser HMS MANXMAN, and the odd submarine which called in with supplies from time to time. The amount of supplies a submarine could carry was very limited in relation to the island's requirements, so something had to be done.

WESTCOTT was in Gibraltar waiting to have repairs done to her boilers, but, nevertheless, she was sent out in this desperate attempt to relieve this small island under siege. The escort consisted of the aircraft carrier HMS EAGLE, three cruisers and ten destroyers. A convoy was to leave the Eastern Mediterranean as we were leaving the Western end. Thus it was hoped to split up the Axis air and naval forces. At the very least a few ships might get through. The whole operation was code-named "Harpoon".

Reflect and have a though for those poor merchant seamen. Their lot was not to be envied. Indeed, it was the merchant seamen that were taking the brunt of all the naval operations. No praise was too high.

On the evening of that day, just off Skirki Bank, the convoy encountered yet another air attack. During this raid three merchant ships were sunk and the cruiser HMS LIVERPOOL was hit in the engine room by a torpedo. All the midship gun-crew on the starboard side were killed. The crane used for lifting her spotter aircraft from the water hung over the side like a drunken man. The ship came to a full stop. HMS ANTELOPE and HMS WESTCOTT were detached to escort her back to Gibraltar. Soon, work commenced aboard LIVERPOOL to try and repair some of the damage. The crane was cut off and pushed over the side. Some of the crew were on the fo'c's'le preparing to be towed. WESTCOTT, because she had only one boiler, was in no position to tow, so ANTELOPE was given the task. When towing arrangements had been completed the long, slow journey back to Gibraltar commenced with WESTCOTT acting as escort.

On Sunday June 14th around daybreak, a single plane was seen circling around us and then made off. We then knew that our plight was recognised and that every endeavour would be made to finish us off. The air attacks that followed can be best summed up from extracts of the ship's log.

1033 First attack from high-level and torpedo bombers.
1600 Four dive-bombers attack.
1808 Ten high-level bombers attack.
1812 One four-engine bomber attacked.
1900 WESTCOTT shoots down one torpedo bomber.
2023 Five high-level bombers attack.
2030 Finally one high-level bomber attacked.

Every time we were under a torpedo-bomber attack, ANTELOPE slipped her tow in order she could better protect LIVERPOOL. It was during one of these torpedo-bomber attacks that our crew Oerlikon gun managed to shoot down one of them and a great cheer went up. Unfortunately, the following day, when three torpedo-bombers were coming in, disaster struck WESTCOTT. Although LIVERPOOL was badly damaged, she still maintained fire power on most of her guns and as one of the low flying planes swept past WESTCOTT a salvo of shells from the LIVERPOOL burst around WESTCOTT. The result was three of our men killed and several injured. One was an eighteen year old seaman on his first voyage, another a seaman off A gun, and the third was the EA who was just leaving the engine room hatch when shrapnel practically cut of his legs and he died from loss of blood.

How LIVERPOOL survived was nothing short of a miracle. Torpedoes continually missed and there were times when she was completely hidden from view by the spray from bombs exploding in the water around her. Both destroyers had narrow escapes too. Fortunately some of the torpedoes that were dropped, were released from so high that they came down vertically and exploded on hitting the water. All aircraft torpedoes, launched at the destroyers, were evaded successfully. Shortly, we three ships were at least out of range of the aircraft. It was time to commit the dead to the deep. All hands were mustered on the quarter deck and a service held as those three brave men were slid silently into the water. I said a special prayer for the EA who was a good friend to me. Soon we were approaching Gibraltar and the faithful tug THAMES came out, taking LIVERPOOL in tow.

Later, we were given to understand that while the aircraft were attacking us none were attacking the main convoy. So it must be assumed the enemy concentrated on the easier target. For a time, at least, they got some respite and continued on their way until reaching the Narrows between Sicily and Tunisia which were heavily mined. So, along with the enemy aircraft, our ships now had mines to contend with and, later, E-boats. By the time Malta was reached only one merchant ship berthed and none of the ships from the Eastern Med. arrived.

Back in dock, LIVERPOOL's underwater hatches were opened up and the dreadful remains of about twenty seamen were found, drowned. Thus was completed another grim tale of a Malta convoy.

The following morning, a number of trawlers and WESTCOTT left Gibraltar at 0600 hours and proceeded out to sea to bury the dead of HMS LIVERPOOL. I presume we went out so early to hide the fact from the Spanish before they arrived on the Rock to get to their work. It was not a pleasant day for us, but all were committed to the deep with the respect and dignity the occasion demanded.

A few days later the auction of the dead sailors' effects took place. Shipmates would bid extravagant sums for each article in order that the dead man's dependants would receive as much as possible to tide them over their bereavement. This was also to show that we cared about their sad loss. For instance, one would buy a hat or shoes knowing full well they would not fit, and return them to the auction for resale. Items would be sold over and over again, thus building up a nice little sum.

The following day, we were out once more in the Mediterranean, on patrol, when we came across a dead airman in the water. He must have been in the water for days and his flying suit was skin tight on him. We lowered the boat, rowed out to him, removed his dog tally (identity disc) from around his neck and attached weights to him. He was left to go down to his watery grave for there was nothing more we could do.

On arriving in harbour the skipper cleared lower decks and read out the awards that had been granted for our part played while escorting the LANGIGGBY CASTLE and Operation Harpoon. The skipper got the DSO and Bar, there were two DSC's, twelve DSM's, and twenty "mentioned in dispatches". During the Sunday morning service, the captain, Commander

Bockett-Pugh, said that as we had all worked together as a team, the awards belonged equally to us all.

The next trip into the Mediterranean was to be my last as I was due to be drafted to HMS CORMORANT, the base ship at Gibraltar.

I walked slowly down the gang plank to the shore. As I did, I reflected on my past years aboard WESTCOTT. You tend to remember the good times and forget the bad, of which there were many.

The good times can be summed up as companionship with your mates, the good runs ashore, and the cameraderie of the messdeck. All the captains and officers I served under were well respected.

The China Station was an experience that I was lucky to know - it could never be repeated. Thanks to the Royal Navy I saw places and met people from different cultures and amassed many memories. Many of the things I saw and did were beyond the comprehension of most people, for which I will always be truly grateful.

On the minus side were the cramped conditions, the lack of fresh food - even bread was a luxury and unobtainable after two days at sea. There were no bathing facilities. Your mess was your bedroom, kitchen,dining room,laundry,and recreation room. We slept in hammocks like sardines in a tin, head to tail, and was about as healthy an environment as the hold of a slave ship! But rat-and-cockroach infested as it was, with condensation dripping off the bulkheads of the ships's side, it was HOME for the best part of a couple of hundred sailors and preferable to the heaving ocean that lay beyond those thin bulkheads!

So with a final wave and farewell I said goodbye to my old ship, WESTCOTT.

CHAPTER TWELVE
Operation Pedestal.

On July 1st, whilst on patrol, WESTCOTT, along with ANTELOPE, arrested three Spanish fishing boats - SEGUARDO, PRIMIER ERRIQUE, and MARIA LUISA, off the Great Shoal Bank in a position close to convoy HG85. Two of these vessels were found to have aboard very powerful W/T and HF W/T equipment and it was thought that these supposed "neutrals" were passing the positions of Allied convoys to the German U-boats. They were arrested and taken into Gibraltar thus, most probably, saving a lot of Allied shipping and men's' lives. WESTCOTT continued patrolling in the Mediterranean until August when she took part in what was the largest convoy of the war.

This great convoy, code-named 'Operation 'Pedestal' was a force of seventy-five warships and one hundred and eighty aircraft to escort fourteen merchant ships to Malta. In addition to the Fleet Air Arm there were about fifty aircraft from the Royal Air Force. These were to be deployed against enemy shipping and air bases.

Lined up against this mighty force was one just as mighty. Available to the Axis Powers was a force consisting of sixty-three warships, five hundred aircraft and two huge minefields.

Although the number of ships to be escorted was small in comparison to an Atlantic convoy, the dangers were much greater. The powers-that-be decided that the need was so important that the relief of Malta was a 'must'. This convoy had to get through!

The British Force consisted of the battle cruiser HMS RODNEY, the battleship HMS NELSON, five aircraft carriers, three light anti-aircraft cruisers, four cruisers, thirty four destroyers, seven corvettes, four minesweepers, nine submarines, seven motor launches and the tug JAUNTY. To complete the quota, there were fourteen merchant ships and three fleet oilers; a total of ninety-three ships.

The convoy itself had an escort of three A A cruisers, twelve destroyers, four mine sweepers, seven motor launches and the tug. There was an escort for the three oilers, HMS WESTCOTT being one of them. There were also escorts for each aircraft carrier. The remainder formed the Battle Fleet ready to take on the Italian Fleet, if it appeared.

The enemy had three heavy cruisers, three light cruisers, twelve destroyers, twenty-one submarines, and twenty-three motor torpedo boats, (E boats) sixty three all together, along with five hundred aircraft operating from Sardinia and Sicily.

As soon as WESTCOTT reached its station the skipper cleared lower deck. Through the loud hailer system he informed all on board of our mission and what was expected of them.

Off Algiers, HMS EAGLE was hit by four torpedoes fired by U-73, under the command of Kapitan Lieutenant Helmut Rosenbaum, for which he received Germany's highest award, the 'Iron Cross'.

WESTCOTTS's crew on deck watched as men ran over the bottom of the ill-fated ship and jumped into the water. What could not be seen was the bravery of some of those men, especially the doctor who, regardless of the danger to himself, administered morphine to those injured, swimming from raft to raft until he was picked up by one of the destroyers. The destroyer, HMS LOOKOUT, to which I had now been drafted, HMS LAFOREY, and the tug JAUNTY were engaged in collecting survivors.

LOOKOUT alone picked up over 500 survivors including Captain L.D. Mackintosh DSC, RN. As LOOKOUT raced to the scene, along with the cruiser HMS CHARYBDIS, they made an unsuccessful depth charge attack on a submarine. The survivors off EAGLE were transferred to HMS VENOMOUS. Shortly afterwards, the aircraft carrier HMS FURIOUS, having completed her task of flying-off aircraft to Malta, and HMS ARGUS, found it too difficult to manoeuvre, and with five destroyers as escort, returned to Gibraltar along with all the men off EAGLE.

The following day on August 12th 1942, the destroyer HMS WOLVERINE got a radar contact on a submarine. She went into attack, rammed and sank it. We all thought it might be the one that had sunk EAGLE, but, unfortunately, it was not. From the survivors WOLVERINE picked up it was found to be an Italian Submarine, DAGABUR. Because of extensive damage to the bows of WOLVERINE when raming the submarine at twenty-six knots, she too had to return to Gibraltar. At the same time, the fleet oilers had completed their task of fuelling all the ships that required oil and had also returned to Gibraltar. The convoy was now reduced to sixty-nine warships.

Shortly afterwards, enemy aircraft appeared and the first air attack started, continuing all day. During any quiet spells submarines attacked. During one of these quiet spells HMS ITHURIEL sighted one on the surface which she rammed and sank. Later, we found it was another Italian submarine, COBALTO.

Aircraft were attacking all day long - there seemed to be hundreds of them. It was safer aboard one of the smaller warships, for the bombers were directing their efforts towards the larger ones and the merchant fleet. Before the merchant ships had left the British Isles they had been fitted with A.A. guns. In fact they had better A.A. defences than many of the escort. The big difference was speed and manoeuvring ability. Two or three of these merchant ships were American, but British army and naval gunners were provided to man and operate the guns of all merchant ships in the convoy.

The anti-aircraft barrages put up were formidable and for a good while all ships proceeded on their way nicely but, at the same time, a sharp watch was kept for those elusive submarines. About a hundred aircraft came in at a time. After they had gone a further wave would come in. The Fleet Air Arm from the carriers were doing a marvellous job, getting quite a score to their credit, as were the ships in the convoy. It could not last, however, as the men on the ships were getting jittery and had started firing on our own aircraft.

Identification signals were either being mis-read or missed altogether, so that when the R.A.F. came to help and protect us they too were fired upon and were soon making a quick retreat back to Malta. The usual thing in the Royal Navy was that all aircraft were the enemy, as we so rarely ever saw our own. Co-operation between the services seemed to be nil at times. The Army had the same problem too.

Around 1830hrs came a very heavy attack and the destroyer, HMS FORESIGHT, was hit by an aerial torpedo. HMS TARTAR went to her assistance and took her in tow. At 2200hrs the situation became uncontrollable so TARTAR took off the survivors, sank FORESIGHT, and returned to Gibraltar.

Meanwhile, WESTCOTT was still in the middle of it when the aircraft carrier, HMS INDOMITABLE, started being hit by bombs from Stuka dive-bombers. The cruiser, HMS CHARYBDIS, the Tribal Class destroyer, HMS SOMALI, and the L Class destroyers, HMS LIGHTNING and LOOKOUT, were detached to assist and protect her.

LOOKOUT went alongside and, although INDOMITABLE dwarfed her, did her best to put out the fires when manning all hoses. After an hour or two she retired gratefully, relieved that she would not have to take the carrier's crew on board, as had been done with EAGLE. The fires were out and INDOMITABLE was able to pick up speed. Soon she was making twenty knots, but her flight-deck looked like a screwed-up sardine can. Her aircraft had to land on the carrier HMS VICTORIOUS, or fly on to Malta because space was at a premium aboard VICTORIOUS.

Within an hour the convoy had reached the Narrows, a stretch of water between Sicily and Tunisia. Here the Italians had heavily mined the waters from one side to the other, so yet another obstacle had to be overcome.

Destroyers formed up with mine-sweeping gear to sweep a channel for the convoy to go through. This was just the beginning of their tribulations for now they would be restricted to the amount of room they would have in which to manoeuvre.

It was at this point 'Z Force', the Battle Fleet, retired as planned. They started to patrol off the North African coast waiting for the Italian Fleet, but it failed to appear.

The following day the damaged ships, ITHURIEL and INDOMITABLE, along with the battle cruiser, HMS RODNEY, which had boiler trouble, and six destroyers, including WESTCOTT, as escort, returned to Gibraltar.

As Y Force was proceeding through the Narrows it was sighted by the Italian submarine AXUM, which fired a salvo of four torpedoes and made four hits. The tanker OHIO was hit, but was able to continue. HMS NIGERIA was hit by one torpedo and fifty-two men were killed. She was unable to carry on and was sent back to Gibraltar. HMS CAIRO was hit by two torpedoes and lost twenty-three men. She was so badly damaged that she was sunk by HMS DERWENT after all survivors had been taken off.

Two of the major A.A. ships had now gone, but the convoy continued on its way. Attacks now came from Italian motor torpedo-boats. During one of these attacks HMS MANCHESTER was hit and so badly damaged she had to be scuttled. The crew took to the boats, and got safely to French North Africa. Thirteen died aboard her and the remainder of the crew were treated very badly by Vichy French. By this time several merchant ships had been hit and their speed reduced to about five knots. Those that were still able to, steamed on, leaving the damaged ones with a small destroyer escort. HMS KENYA was then torpedoed by the Italian submarine, ALAGI. Three men unfortunately were killed in this attack. The convoy was now in complete disarray, but still it continued to Malta the best way it could with what ships that were left.

Of the fourteen merchant ships that set off, nine were sunk. The five that got through to Malta were all damaged. Those that got through were ROCHESTER CASTLE, MELBOURNE STAR, BRISBANE STAR, PORT CHALMERS and the tanker OHIO. OHIO arrived in Grand Harbour held up between two destroyers. OHIO carried aviation fuel which was a godsend for Malta's air defence. From the remaining merchant ships thirty-two thousand tons of cargo was unloaded, which saved Malta.

By the time the convoy reached Malta they had gone through the heaviest air attack known on a British Fleet, in which about five hundred enemy aircraft took part. A concentrated attack of twenty-nine submarines and twenty-three E-boats plus two large mine-fields had also helped shatter the convoy. Royal Naval losses were high. Four warships had been sunk, six damaged and two hundred and eighty-eight men killed. The Fleet Air Arm lost twenty-nine aircraft including those that were on board HMS EAGLE. The R.A.F. lost five.

While all this was taking place our submarines were on the lookout for the elusive Italian Fleet. When the submarine, HMS UNBROKEN, came upon four cruisers and eight destroyers the Captain immediately commenced an attack and fired his torpedoes. He hit the heavy cruiser BOLZANO and the light cruiser MUZIO ATTENDOLO, but was unable to press home the attack because of the heavy concentration of destroyers. The Italians then withdrew to their home ports.

The enemy lost two submarines, COBALTO and DAGABUR, forty-three aircraft, and two cruisers were damaged, one of which never put to sea again.

Although many of our men and ships were lost, Malta had been saved and this became the turning point of the war.

On the 15th August 1942 the returning Z Force reached Gibraltar. "Operation Pedestal" had been completed.

Capt. Brian De Courcey-Ireland
as a Sub-Lieutenant aboard Westcott
after the Armistice in 1918

Capt. Brian De Courcey-Ireland
aged 94 at the 1994 HMS Westcott
reunion at the Union Jack Club

CHAPTER THIRTEEN

Operation Torch.

WESTCOTT continued patrolling in the Atlantic and Mediterranean and on one sunny morning, while returning to Gibraltar in the company of the destroyers VIDETT, ITHURIEL and PARTRIDGE, one lonely corvette was witnessed coming towards them. Suddenly the corvette started firing depth charges and, to their surprise, a U-boat surfaced. A ring was formed around her and WESTCOTT closed in.

The Germans were pouring out of the conning tower and forming an orderly line along its deck. Obviously they were surrendering. Then suddenly one of the ships in the group opened fire with a machine gun. WESTCOTT's captain, Commander Bocket-Pugh ordered them to cease fire immediately. He was livid that someone had stupidly taken this action. Not only were we in danger of receiving cross-fire but it was totally unnecessary, irresponsible and a disgraceful act that brought discredit to the Royal Navy code of ethics.

German sailors were falling in the water and an officer in the conning tower slumped downwards as he was hit by bullets.

WESTCOTT was very close to the U-boat and as she withdrew they watched it suddenly sink beneath the flat calm sea. Sea cocks had no doubt been opened before the decision to surrender. Survivors were picked up. Not a pleasant incident.

The next phase in the war was the landings in North Africa.

November 6th saw the start of Operation Torch. Troops were to be landed at Casablanca, Oran and Algiers. The Americans were to land at Casablanca, the British at Algiers and combined forces at Oran. A huge force of landing craft and supply ships left Britain and America to converge on North Africa in order to land simultaneously. When this had been accomplished, our united forces would move east to meet the 8th Army, thus squeezing the Germans out of North Africa.

With the opening of the campaign at El Alamein and the landings to the West, the Axis armies and the Luftwaffe were being stretched to their limit. The siege of Malta had now been lifted and the island airfields could be used by our Air Force. This created more headaches for Rommel, the German commander.

The Vichy French had two battle-cruisers, one battleship, seven cruisers, twenty-four destroyers and sixteen submarines in Toulon. The Italians had at least as many at Taranto and other ports. H Force, the covering force, consisted of the battle-cruisers HMS RODNEY and RENOWN, the battleships HMS DUKE OF YORK, NELSON, VALIANT and WARSPITE, with the battleships HMS HOWE and KING GEORGE V in reserve. The force also consisted of the aircraft-carriers HMS ILLUSTRIOUS, VICTORIOUS and FORMIDABLE. There were two heavy cruisers, ten light cruisers and thirty-two destroyers.

WESTCOTT's role in this armada was to join up with the transport ships and escort them to their destination.

This incredible array of ships seemed to stretch far away onto the horizon. There were over five hundred transport ships carrying tens of thousands of American troops and protected by three hundred and fifty naval vessels, mainly from the British Navy.

WESTCOTT was given the task of supporting two coast-guard cutters, HMS HARTLAND and WALMER, whose bows had been reinforced to allow them to crash through the boom defence at the entrance to Oran harbour and then take over the harbour defences.

While going through the straits of Gibraltar one of the coast-guard cutters developed engine trouble, so it was decided that WESTCOTT might have to take her place in the onslaught. WESTCOTT rushed into Gibraltar to unload all confidential papers, etc., in case she was captured in Oran harbour.

On rejoining HARTLAND and WALMER, most of WESTCOTT's crew were relieved to learn that the cutter's engine trouble had been rectified.

Under cover of darkness, on 7th November, WESTCOTT approached Oran harbour. All the town lights were on and car headlights could be seen in the hills above. It seemed that our impending visit was totally unexpected.

On the stroke of midnight HARTLAND and WALMER made a dash for the harbour. Men on board watched with bated breath as those two brave ships crashed into the boom and all hell broke loose. The noise of gunfire was intense then, suddenly,

WESTCOTT was caught in the full glare of one of them and was immediately fired upon. Luckily, their aim wasn't very accurate. Tracer bullets sped towards her, but they fell short. Then shells whined overhead. Luckily, for WESTCOTT, some of the heavy ships out at sea opened fire on the searchlights and gun emplacements in the hills and all the searchlights were extinguished.

Meanwhile, fighting went on in the harbour, where HARTLAND and WALMER fought to the end. Many men were killed and injured and the remainder taken captive, but the brave crews of these two gallant ships had completed their mission. The survivors were not prisoners for long as the American and British had landed troops on either side of Oran and had soon captured the town. WESTCOTT expected to be ordered to join in the fight, but instead, was ordered to head for the open sea.

On 8th November 1942 WESTCOTT's Asdics detected a submarine. Going into attack she depth-charged and sank it, in position 36 degrees 48 minutes North, 00 degrees 59 minutes West. It was later discovered the submarine was the Vichy submarine ACTAEON.

Shortly afterwards on November 18th WESTCOTT left Gibraltar, escorting HMS DUKE OF YORK and the aircraft carrier HMS VICTORIOUS back to the U.K.

Meanwhile the landings were still proceeding and positions were consolidated. It was not known at the time whether the French would team up with the Axis powers or not. The French in North West Africa were certainly hostile towards the

Meanwhile the landings were still proceeding and positions were consolidated. It was not known at the time whether the French would team up with the Axis powers or not. The French in North West Africa were certainly hostile towards the British. H Force was required to prevent any attack on our landing forces. If the French and Italians decided to join forces there certainly would have been one almighty battle.

A short time later the Germans tried to force their way into Toulon to get the French Fleet. The French had resisted but to no avail, so they had scuttled their own ships and destroyed the harbour, thus preventing the Germans from gaining a Mediterranean Fleet to attack us. When the C in C, Admiral Sir Andrew Cunningham, heard of this he decided to use his Fleet to help with the landings. It was learned later that at Oran and Algiers the British forces were dressed as Americans in the hope the French would think they were Yanks, probably saving a lot of lives. Another reason was for propaganda purposes for American consumption in the U.S. and to let the Japanese know that the Americans were strong enough to fight on all fronts.

Algiers was the first to fall with Oran shortly afterwards and, finally, Casablanca. Good news was coming in fast and soon the British and Americans were fighting their way towards the 8th Army.

CHAPTER FOURTEEN

To Russia with Love!

Between December 14th 1942 and July 19th 1943 HMS WESTCOTT was at Portsmouth undergoing a refit and being altered to a long range escort (LRE) for duty on Russian convoys.

While this work was in progress the ship had been decommissioned and those left on board formed a skeleton crew of eight men for care and maintenance. After the work had been completed the ship was recommissioned with a new crew to face the diabolical conditions which those who had gone before her had done. Only this crew had to face the reality that the only certain fact that if not killed in action and the ship sank they'd be certain to die in those cold arctic waters. Not a very pleasant prospect and certainly a daunting mission. To add to the pleasures of their life afloat were the awful conditions on board. The food situation was usually critical and a good hot meal would have been a great treat but we had to rely largely on the old faithful kye and corned beef. During those days, there were no bread-baking facilities, no refrigerators, no freezers and good food of any description was in short supply. The captain occasionally would get the duty Asdic rating to search for a shoal of fish, drop a depth charge among them, and then scoop up the victims using buckets. No way would a boat be lowered in those forbidding waters. One day they caught a huge conger eel which was immediately skinned and cut into steaks to make a memorable gastronomic treat for all.

The mountainous waves of the North Atlantic even dwarfed the larger ships in the convoy. For a small destroyer and her crew, they were of nightmare proportions. At times nobody was allowed on the upper deck. Stokers and seamen alike were forbidden to leave their duty stations, sometimes for more than twelve hours, owing to the perilous weather. Those treacherous Russian convoys will never be forgotten in the minds of the men that experience them.

And so we come to the narrative written by Captain S Farquharson-Roberts RN who was navigating officer aboard WESTCOTT at the time. It is written in a form of a log of one of those unforgettable convoys.

> "22.1.44
>
> JW56B and RA56 37 ships. Back departure 3.2.44 arrival Loch Ewe 11.2.44 (Roskill).
>
> After a very tiring night spent at action stations, dragging the anchor, we proceeded across Loch Ewe to find a more sheltered billet. The wind moderated slightly and one began to wonder whether conditions were fair enough to put to sea. The disadvantage of doing so was a debatable matter. We would have greatly liked a good night in before leaving harbour (the previous night being less of a night in than one would even get at sea) but on the other hand the convoy had already been delayed several days on account of the weather and prevailing opinion was "Lets get the evil business over and done with"

Wishful thinking was brought to an end however when the Commodore hoisted his 'Weigh and Proceed' signal. Since we were the Senior Officer for the opening stages we had to be out with the leading ship, which was rather annoying as it always means hanging around for hours outside until the convoy forms up.

Heavy seas were encountered as soon as we left Loch Ewe. Not a propitious start. Coming up suddenly the weather caused nearly half the ship's company to succumb to sea sickness. Thanks to the doctors pills I was among the happier half.

After the usual stooging around, while the convoy joined up, we took up station ahead and proceeded to Iceland. For some days past, grim signals had been coming in, an extremely severe gale had broken up the convoy ahead of us and we soon passed one or two ships which had to leave and subsequently turn back, JA56A (Roskill).

The expected seldom happens however and we struck nothing worse than a heavy swell and a force 6 wind from the SW; quite normal for these waters.

25.1.44.

Two uneventful days passed in the convoy and we picked up land echoes by radar at long range on the morning of the 25th. As we had to fuel at Suddisfjord we left convoy behind at 1000hrs and carried on at 18 knots.

During the afternoon a local offshore wind picked up, quickly becoming a force 8 gale and lashing the sea up until we had to reduce speed on account of the heavy bumping. One advantage of being in these old destroyers is that one has to take care of them more than the fleet destroyers in heavy seas, since their old plates cannot stand up to much without the rivets beginning to loosen. Consequently it never becomes too uncomfortable. During the afternoon a fleet destroyer which had unsuccessfully tried to meet us eight hours earlier went past at 20 knots and at times gave a very realistic imitation of a submarine.

It was bitterly cold and the spray froze almost before it hit the bridge, so we were soon iced up on the standing rigging and fo'castle guard rails.

We entered Suddisfjord about 1630 and went straight alongside the oiler. After a while the WHITEHALL came alongside and we were able to take a few drinks together and wish each other luck before the long trip started.

We slipped at 2200 and proceeded to rejoin the convoy, first securing the ship in anticipation of heavy weather. Once again we met the unexpected, the wind dropped and a brilliant aurora was playing over a clear blue sky. We picked up the convoy without difficulty, taking up station well ahead until daylight afforded us better chance of sorting things out.

26.1.44

The 3rd destroyer flotilla joined the convoy as expected next forenoon and we took up position on the port quarter of the convoy. The convoy now had a formidable escort of six fleet destroyers, twelve V and W destroyers, several fleet sweepers and some corvettes, far more than would be found on any Atlantic convoy. This is probably due to the possibility of interference by the TIRPITZ in Kola fjord or a flotilla of German destroyers.

26.1.44

During the day a sea swell subsided, the wind dropped and for once it was quite pleasant to be on the job. Calm weather means increased enemy activity however, so we were not surprised to see an un-identified aircraft during the afternoon at extreme range - probably a 'J.U.88' making preliminary reports of the convoy movements. It soon disappeared and we rightly surmised that we had been spotted and reported to the Germans. This meant probable return of the aircraft next day to check up our speed and possibly start homing the U-boats and other aircraft homing in on us.

27.1.44

Sure enough at 1300 the next day he was back again, a bit bolder this time. Coming within range of one or two of the heavier armed ships. (He would have to be close indeed to come within effective range of our two four inch guns) However hope springs eternal and we closed up at air action stations on the off chance. By now it was quite clear the enemy knew all about us and from other information received we knew that several U-boats were converging on us. Reports from the convoy ahead indicated that they had been through a heavy attack three merchant ships had been sunk and one escort damaged. This afforded us one consolation in that at least six U-boats had had their stings drawn and would be going home for new ones.

28.1.44.

The convoy ahead reached their destination the next day and we were very pleased to hear that the 26th destroyer flotilla was doing a quick turn around and coming back to help us. The U-boats would now have a very tough nut to crack, with such a strong support group patrolling around the convoy, leaving a strong screen intact.

Meanwhile the general situation pointed to an attack by U-boats not before the 29th for they do not attack as they arrive, but wait and form up into a pack some way off first. On the other hand large scale air attack with glider bombs and other horrors was quite on the cards for the 28th.

28.1.44

But the air attack never came, possibly they are running short of aircraft in other outposts of their ill-gotten

Empire. Instead, the normal shadow turned up punctually at 1300 a 'B.V.138' this time. He stayed about an hour.

29.1.44.

Now for it? R.T. silence had been broken all ships were on top line at 1000 on the 29th we saw and heard heavy gun fire on the horizon by the starboard quarter of the convoy. The report soon came over the air WHITEHALL and MAHRATTA were engaging two surface U boats. WHITEHALL again! she always seems to have the fun. No jealousies are as strong as family ones, as in the case here her Skipper Lieutenant Commander Cowell is my second cousin-in-law. A few minutes later both U-boats had dived, no hits had been observed and the two destroyers proceeded to sit on 'em gradually dropping astern. Soon the distant rumble of depth charges which were to be heard almost incessantly for the next three days announcing headaches, at least, for two U-boat crews. Even if the depth charges do not prove fatal they achieve the chief aim of preventing the submarines concerned from taking any further part in the operation. For although the hulls take a lot of cracking electric light bulbs and already frayed nerves don't.

On the strength of this excitement we had gone to action stations, which was just as well as a couple of shadowing 'B.V.138's decided to have a really close look at us. This gave us a long awaited chance to open fire, but it was an abortive shoot. The rounds falling into the water at short range. Still it achieved the purpose of making the planes keep their distance. We switched to defence watches (one in two instead of one in three) so as to have both guns manned, but apart from WHITEHALL and MAHRATTA's continued attacks, nothing further happened during the afternoon and the convoy arrived safely in Kola on the 2.2.44. Returning with 37 ships on the 3rd February, arriving at Loch Ewe on the 11th February 1944.

On the 27.3.44 WESTCOTT escorted JW 58 from Loch Ewe and arrived at Kola on 5.2.44 with no losses and returned with RA 58 from Kola on the 7.4.44 arriving back to Loch Ewe on the 14th April 1944."

So ends the narrative written by Captain S Farquarson-Roberts RN Ret

Finally we present a contribution from ex-Signalman 'Stormy' Fairweather, who joined WESTCOTT in January 1944.

"I arrived at Glasgow railway station after a long tedious journey from Chatham. There were three others on the same draft as me and while awaiting our transport down to the docks where WESTCOTT was berthed we adjourned to the nearest pub where I had my very first pint of 'Black and Tan'. After three pints of this nectar we were called to our transport. By the time we reached Greenock I was a little worse for wear. However, toting my bag and hammock I somehow managed to negotiate two gang planks and follow directions to my mess, which was down a hatchway in the seamen's messdeck to what was to be my home for the next eighteen months. Number three mess.

I found a billet from which to sling my hammock and was very glad to turn in; to be awakened next morning to find that we were at sea and the ship beginning to pitch and roll. It was not long before this started taking its toll on my stomach and soon I was hanging over the side; but at least I was not alone.

Fortunately the trip was not a long one before we arrived at Loch Ewe where a convoy was assembled. It was only a short respite for we were soon off again. (So was my stomach) I soon found out that we were on our way to Russia, escorting convoy JW56B, consisting of seventeen merchant ships. The destroyer HARDY was torpedoed by U278. There were no other losses. U314 was sunk by WHITEHALL and METEOR.

This was the first of five Russian convoys that I was to experience. On one, a U-boat was reported on the surface, so we, in company with another destroyer (which I believe was WHITEHALL) gave chase at full speed. The old tub shook like a pneumatic drill. The yeoman shouted to we signalmen on the flag deck "Hook up enemy in sight and the Battle Ensign". After a short while with his telescope to his eye he shouted to the captain "Enemy in sight, sir!" and to us, "Hoist!" Up went the flags. I believe the yeoman got a Mention in Despatches for that. It was not long before we could all see the U-boat through our binoculars, then the cry went up, "She's about to dive sir!" By this time a gun was trained on her and the skipper shouted, "Open fire!" The U-boat was at extreme range. The gunnery officer, sub lieutenant Trevor Riches, on the gun deck platform repeated the order, when the peak of his cap fell off! But what a good shot. It was very close and just fell short. On arriving at the position where she dived we carried out a depth charge attack for some time but could not confirm a 'kill'.

During a respite from convoy duties in Kola inlet on which stands the port of Murmansk, we were tied up alongside at Polyarno. The weather was fine and we held a regatta. All ships taking part. We had escorted the U.S. cruiser MILWAUKEE to be handed over to the North Russian Fleet. It was quite good fun and WESTCOTT was 'Tote' ship. So we signalmen were kept busy sending out the betting odds and numbers of boats taking part etc.

It was while here I set foot for the first time on Russian soil, but alas, we were not allowed outside the dockyard area. I remember the Russian army women carrying fixed bayonets, which they looked quite prepared to use if we had tried to get out of the dock area.

On the return trip we had Russian sailors in our mess taking passage to the U.K. to man ships that we had given them. I believe they were the old four funnel, top-heavy destroyers that the U.S had given us in exchange for bases in the Far East. From the stories heard from some who had sailed in them I bet our blokes were glad to give them away.

On the 3rd of June 1944 we were all given a pamphlet from General Eisenhower telling of the great crusade that we were about to embark upon. So we sailed from Greenock and soon met up with the battleships WARSPITE and RAMILLES with the intention of escorting them to the French coast to bombard the shore batteries, but because of adverse weather conditions we had to sail around in circles, waiting until the weather was right for the invasion fleet to set sail.

At dawn on "D Day" the battleships set about silencing any shore batteries and troop movements. What a din! What fire power! The very next day WESTCOTT developed a split in one of her boilers and as no "lame ducks" were wanted in the area we were sent back to the Solent to effect emergency repairs.

As we passed through the many ships that lay at anchor they all sounded their sirens etc., welcoming us back. After dropping anchor, I was duty signalman on the bridge and noticed a light flashing our pennant number. On answering it I found it to be my eldest brother who was serving on an MTB! Of course, there was no chance of any meeting, for it was not long before we were away again. This time patrolling the French coast on our own. It was whilst there I celebrated my eighteenth birthday with 'sippers' all round. I remember Les Lawrence bringing me a mug full of 'neaters' whilst I was on the flag deck. That was the last I remember until I woke up laying in a coil of rope on the upper deck.

We then went to Dundee to have the boiler fixed, this meant three weeks leave for each watch! While the other watch was on leave I remember some of us being invited to a wedding where there was a shortage of men. We had a wonderful time. My, those Dundee people were very hospitable!

So back to Russian convoys. One of which was a fast one escorting two troop ships, the EMPRESS OF AUSTRALIA and the SCYTHIA, carrying 11,000 Russians captured in Normandy. Their fate is unknown but I doubt whether they were shown any mercy. The British escorts were not allowed alongside nor were we allowed ashore.

The next convoy we escorted was JW62, which was to be the last convoy to Russia for WESTCOTT. The convoy consisted of two aircraft carriers and a cruiser. It arrived in Kola Inlet without loss.

The return convoy RA63 was the last and the worst. It consisted of thirteen merchant ships, the cruiser DIADEM and escort carrier VINDEX. The weather on this convoy was unbelievable with WESTCOTT tossed about like a cork. The only difference was that the cork would have stayed on the water. WESTCOTT was at times almost submerged. All ships had to turn into the wind. One minute WESTCOTT would be perched on top of a wave, the next her bows were pointing down into the tumultuous sea: men were being thrown about and some suffered injuries. I was up on the bridge hanging on for dear life, soaked to the skin and bitterly cold. Down below our sick berth attendant was attending to the injured, he himself sustaining cuts to his head. He was using torn up vests for bandages, this went on for several hours. At last when the storm subsided there was a terrific swell and when WESTCOTT turned to resume her course she keeled over that far I thought for a few seconds she would never return upright: but she did. For a small ship like that to take such a pounding from the sea was a credit to her builders, but she had rivets pulled out of her hull and had to pull into the Faeroes for repairs, before she could continue home. Arriving in Greenock on the 23rd January, a great deal of damage had been done to the superstructure. It was while she keeled over at such an angle and the crew thought it would never return upright, that oil spilled out of the fuel tank in the seaman's mess deck. So to add to their unfortunately plight they had to put up with the stench of oil all the way home. One had to be careful not to break one's neck slipping in it. When we arrived back the task of cleaning up began, which took ages.

After WESTCOTT had been patched up we had a nice little number escorting the ferries between Stranraer and Larne to Northern Ireland and back. We were at Greenock on "VE DAY". The celebrations were wild to say the least. Unfortunately we were anchored out in the Clyde when came the pipe, 'Splice the Main Brace!' The officers, including the skipper, Lieutenant

Commander Reade, came along to the seaman's mess deck bearing bottles of beer etc. The skipper had a black beard and had a cigarette in his mouth, one of the seamen went to give him a light and set fire to his beard! The skipper blamed me and started to chase me threatening to throw me over the side, among other things! Fortunately he never caught me and the incident was forgotten. The next day we received orders to proceed to Iceland. On the way there we came across a number of surrendering U-boats. We gave them instructions to proceed to Campbeltown but had no star shells left to illuminate their route , having fired them all during the previous day's celebrations.

After returning from Iceland we wonder how long it would be before we were demobbed. The first to go was Bill Johnson, another signalman. He was Town Clerk of Doncaster and was required to prepare for the forthcoming General Election. Soon it was farewell to WESTCOTT. A ship I shall never be able to forget! Why? I don't know! Perhaps it was because she was my first ship, my first experience of sea life, or because she had most of my guts." ***Stormy.***

FINALE

On 26th June 1945 WESTCOTT was paid off into Category 'C' Reserve at Barrow. Approval to scrap was given the following month. In April she was sold to the newly nationalised British Iron and Steel Corporation, allocated to

West of Scotland Ship Breaking Co. Ltd and towed from Barrow to be broken up at Troon.

So ends the story of HMS WESTCOTT - twenty-eight tumultuous years of gallant service.

AB Ernie Woods

SPO Allen Flisher

ACKNOWLEDGEMENTS

The author, Tom Chapman, gratefully acknowledges the help received from the following in producing this book.

1. **Captain Brian de Courcy-Ireland** for his World War One information and anecdotes relating to his early days on WESTCOTT.
2. **Allen Flisher** for his memories of joining the China Station aboard WESTCOTT in 1937.
3. **Ernie 'Splinter' Woods** for extracts from his comprehensive records.
4. **Morris Coley** for his water-colour of the 74-gun HMS MAJESTIC commanded by Captain Westcott when sunk at the Battle of the Nile 1798.
5. **Les Lawrence** for his water-colour of HMS WESTCOTT that inspired Sam Morley for the cover design and title of this book.
6. **Sam Morley**, ex HMS VERDUN and HMS REDOUBT, author/publisher of **99 YEARS OF NAVY, DURBAN'S LADY IN WHITE, JUST NUISANCE A.B., BACK TO DURBAN - 50 YEARS ON**, plus eight more non-naval hardbacks, who undertook to edit and design **WATER, WATER EVERY WHERE**, when approached by the author.
7. **Captain S Farquharson-Roberts RN** for his contribution on WESTCOTT's involvement in Arctic convoys in Chapter 13 pages 139 to 145.
8. **'Stormy' Fairweather** for his contribution of WESTCOTT's involvement in Arctic convoys in Chapter 13 pages 145 to 151.

9. **Alison W Duffield** of the Dept of Printed Books at the Imperial War Museum.
10. **Dr R Pope BA PhD** Head of School of Historical and Critical Studies University of Central Lancashire.
11. The author's sons, **Gordon Chapman BA Hons** and **Ronald Chapman**, plus his daughter-in-law **Pauline Chapman** who proof-read and type-set his early text.
12. The many old shipmates, too numerous to name here, who helped fill in the 50-year old gaps in his narrative.

The Author

Captain Farquharson Roberts

Stormy Fairweather

HMS WESTCOTT Shipmates.

CAPTAINS

Lt Cdr C.R. Peploe (1918)
Lt Cdr A.B.D. James(1930)
Cpt Lolly (1936)
Cdr Firth (1938)
Cdr Collie-Hill (1938)
Lt Cdr W. Seagrave (1940)
Cdr W. Bockett-Pugh (1941)
Lt H. Lampton (1943)
Lt Cdr Reade (1946)

OFFICERS

Lt Dr Bill Loughborough
1st Lt McCall
1st Lt Brightman
1st Ltd Ernest Quarrie
Lt W Hawkins
Lt Anderson
Lt Noel Britten
Lt Chadwick
Lt Trevor Riches
Lt Stuart Farquharson-Roberts*
Sub Lt Ted Leathers
Sub Lt Michael Wilson
Sub Lt Brian de Courcy-Ireland *
Warrant Officer Ralph.
*Retired Captain

MEN

Bill Ames
Anderson
Fred Austin
Baker (AB)
G Barber
Tom Bartholomew
Alf Beckett (AB) DSM
Dennis Benfield (AB)
Bennett (Sig)
Ron Blacker (PO)
Sid Blower (AB)

Dennis Borsman (OD)
Bowden (SBA)
Jack Bradshaw (L/S)
A. Burden (L/S)
C Burgin (AB)
Herbert Canham (PO)
Joe Carr (PO Buffer)
Jack Carty (PO Cook)
Joe Catlin (AB)
Tom Chapman (L/S)
George Cheney (AB)
G Clancey (AB)
Nobby Clark (AB)
Bill Clark(AB)
Sid Cloutman (AB)
R Cole
Herbert Clover (AB)
P Cook (Tel)
P Cooper (Tel)
Crane (AB)
Croft (Coder)
Ted Cross (AB)
Harry Dixon (PO)
R Delieu (AB)
C Dowling
Duval (AB)

E Dykes (AB)
Eddie Edwards (AB)
Stormy Fairwater (Sig)
Allen Flisher (SPO)
Foulger (PO)
Frame (AB)
Eddoe Francis (SPO)
W Galloway (AB)
Arthur Gardner (AB)
Garrard (AB)
Garrity (AB)
F George (AB)
D Godfrey (PO Buffer)
J Green (AB)
D Grey
George Hall (AB)
N Hall (Yeoman)
E Humphreys (AB)
Hunt
Jarvis (PO)
T Jenkins (AB)
Bill Johnson (Sig)
J Jolliffe
Eric Kemp (L?S
F King
B Law (AB)
Les Lawrence (Sig)
Thomas Mack
W Manor
Walter Mason
Alf Manning
Pat McKenna (AB)
Jock McKivett (Sig)
Pat McNeil (AB)
Meany (AB)
Bill Merry (L/G STO)
John Mills (Cox) DSM
H Money
George Moore (AB)
Morris (AB)
W Mutlow (Cox)
Len Newton
Arthur Nicholls
George Nicholas
Fred Pacey (Tel)
Parker (AB)
Frank Powell (AB)
George Puslow (AB)
Rance (AB)
L Reed
F Reid
Richardson (PO)
Ted Rodgers (PO)
R Rose
Roy Ross (AB)
Bob Smale (L/G Sig
Ginger Sawyers (Tel)
Sam Simmons
Studwick
C Swinburn
Sykes (AB)
H Taylor (AB)
H Thurtle
Harry Townsend (L/S)
R Turnbull (AB)
Les Turner (AB)
Jim Underwood (L/S)
Waller (AB)
Watts (AB)
J Wells (STO)
F Wheatley
Roy Wilkinson
Ernie Woods (AB)
Wright (AB)

INDEX

(merchant ships in capitals)